Rawmazing

Over 130 Simple Raw Recipes for Radiant Health

Rawmazing

Over 130 Simple Raw Recipes for Radiant Health

Susan Powers

Photography by Susan Powers

Skyhorse Publishing

Skyhorse Publishing books may be purchased in bulk at special discounts for sales promotion, corporate gifts, fund-raising, or educational purposes.
Special editions can also be created to specifications. For details, contact the Special Sales Department, Skyhorse Publishing, 307 West 36th Street, 11th Floor, New York, NY 10018 or info@skyhorsepublishing.com.

Skyhorse® and Skyhorse Publishing® are registered trademarks of Skyhorse Publishing, Inc.®, a Delaware corporation.

www.skyhorsepublishing.com

10 9 8 7 6 5 4 3 2

Library of Congress Cataloging-in-Publication Data

Powers, Susan.
 Rawmazing : easy raw food / Susan Powers ; photography by Susan Powers.
    p. cm.
 ISBN 978-1-61608-627-5 (pbk. : alk. paper)
 1. Quick and easy cooking. 2. Raw foods. I. Title.
 TX833.5.P69 2011
 613.2'65--dc23
                        2012001892

Printed in China

To my family, my love for you inspires me daily.
I love you deeply.

To Mary, thank you for all your patience editing this manuscript.

To all the readers of Rawmazing. You continue to amaze me
with your support. Without you, there would be no Rawmazing!

Contents

Introduction

"Food sustains us... Yet what we eat may affect our risk for several of the leading causes of death for Americans, notably, coronary heart disease, stroke, arteriosclerosis, diabetes, and some types of cancer. These disorders together now account for more than two-thirds of all deaths in the United States."

—*Former Surgeon General Dr. C. Everett Koop*

It is estimated that 75 percent of disease is caused by the SAD diet (Standard American Diet). If food is the culprit, I believe that food can be the answer. As we become mindful about what we eat, we can start to make choices that promote our health over illness. Food is consumed for nutrition, but it is also consumed for pleasure. What happens if we learn how to satisfy our pleasure receptors with healthy food? Our lives improve.

What do our bodies need to eat raw?

What are the building blocks that our bodies need to function? Enzymes, vitamins, minerals, phytonutrients, protein, essential fats, and fiber. These are all provided by our food and are involved in growth, repair, and maintenance of the body. Let's take a quick look at each of these and what they do for us.

ENZYMES

Enzymes convert the food we eat into chemical structures that can pass through the membranes of the cells' lining, the digestive tract, and into the blood stream. Their job doesn't end there. Enzymes are the living proteins that direct the life force into our biochemical and metabolic processes. They help transform and store energy, make active hormones, dissolve fiber, and prevent clotting. They have anti-inflammatory effects. Enzymes help balance and restore the immune system, and heal many diseases. Enzymes even help repair our DNA and our RNA.

When we cook food, we destroy many of the enzymes that help us naturally digest it.

VITAMINS

Without vitamins our cells would not function properly and thus our organs would suffer and eventually we would no longer be able to survive. Vitamins help regulate metabolism, help convert fat and carbohydrates into energy, and assist in forming bone and tissue. Guess what happens when you cook food? You got it, a large percentage of the vitamins are destroyed.

Viktoras Kulvinskas, in his book *Survival into the 21st Century*, estimates that the overall nutrient destruction is as high as 80 percent. Tests have shown that we will lose 50 percent of the B vitamins while B1 and B12 can lose up to 96 percent. 97 percent of folic acid is destroyed as well as 70-80 percent of vitamin C.

MINERALS

Seventeen of the thirty elements known to be essential to life are minerals. Mineral deficiencies cause disease in humans. Minerals also have a synergistic relationship with vitamins, working together to improve our health. When foods are cooked, many of the minerals are destroyed or altered, rendering them useless.

PHYTONUTRIENTS

Phytonutrients are what give fruits and vegetables their color. Phytonutrients protect the body and fight disease. They also fight cancer and help your heart. Phytonutrients are at the leading edge of research on nutrition. They provide medicine for cell health. And once again, phytonutrients in freshly harvested plant foods can be destroyed or removed by cooking.

Why Eat Raw?

It just starts to make sense. If cooking destroys the vital and essential nutrients that we need to stay healthy, eating our food raw does the opposite. It provides us with what we need for our health and well-being. I know from experience that when I am eating at least 80 percent raw, I have more energy, more mental focus, and all of the pesky things that irritate me on a daily basis, like acid reflux and my daily aches and pains, dissipate. I also know that I am feeding my body what it needs to thrive, not just survive.

Kitchen Equipment

I often get asked what equipment I have in my raw food kitchen. The following are the items I find helpful and use quite often.

Knives: You can do almost anything you need to do with a good, sharp chopping knife and a paring knife. Your knives are important and worth investing in. Keep them sharp to avoid accidents.

Food Processor: I use a Kitchen Aid food processor. It is my favorite. It is important to note that different food processors have different size motors which means it may take longer for those with smaller motors to get the job done.

Dehydrators: I use the TSM stainless steel dehydrator. Another favorite among raw foodists is the Excalibur. I have both. You want to make sure that your dehydrator has a temperature control.

Spiral Cutter: A good spiral cutter is a great asset for your kitchen. It makes vegetable noodles from all kinds of veggies such as zucchini.

High-Speed Blenders: There are two high-speed blenders that are really worth mentioning. One is the Vitamix and the other is the Blendtec. I have both in my kitchen and they each work very well. The Vitamix relies on a plunger to work with more difficult food while the Blendtec has a variable speed. The Vitamix is a little heavier and more expensive. The Blendtec has a wide jar that is easier to get your food out of.

Magic Bullet Blender: These powerful little blenders work great when you only need to blend a small amount. They are reasonably priced and with the two different blades, are very versatile.

Microplane: Initially developed as a wood working tool, this grater is amazing in the kitchen. You can get them in many different sizes. They quickly grate ginger or garlic or zest lemons and oranges.

Mandoline Slicer: A great way to slice fruits and veggies. You can slice from ¼ inch to paper thin. Check prices. They range from very expensive to inexpensive. Make sure you get one that is easy to slice with and use caution.

Whisk: I have whisks in many sizes in my kitchen. When I am mixing up a quick ganache, there is nothing better. The smaller ones work great when you have small amounts. Make sure you have a small and a medium for starters.

Sprouting Jars: I like to keep a couple of different sizes on hand. These are glass jars with mesh tops that screw on. They make sprouting very easy.

Springform Pans: Spring form pans are wonderful when making cheesecakes and some tarts. They are metal pans that have removable bottoms, making unmoulding very easy.

Tart Pans: I have a large collection of tart pans. These are pans that have fluted edges and removable bottoms. I love the smaller sizes for individual servings and the larger sizes when I want to make a larger tart. They are good for both sweet and savory dishes.

Baking Rings: Baking rings are metal rings that are about 3½ inches in diameter and about 3 inches tall. They are great when making stacked food.

Helpful Hints

Dehydration: In the raw food world, the dehydrator is your oven. It is a very versatile piece of equipment that allows you to make "baked" items without destroying the vitamins, minerals, enzymes, and other nutrients that occur naturally in our food.

The dehydrator works by circulating warm air around food. By keeping the temperature below 116 degrees, we keep the nutrients in the food intact. The dehydrator opens the door to gourmet raw food, allowing endless menu possibilities. Veggie chips, eggplant "bacon," burgers, breads, and crackers are just some of the treats you will discover.

The most important thing to remember with dehydration is that the food temperature needs to stay under 116 degrees. You will notice that many times (not every), I start dehydration at a higher temperature and then reduce the temperature after an hour. Many people question if this is still considered raw. Rest assured, it is. The food temperature is what we are concerned with here, and in that first hour, the food being dehydrated is only kicking off moisture. The food temperature never goes over 115 degrees. Just remember to turn the temperature down after the initial time period. Setting a kitchen timer is the easiest way to do this.

There are quite a few benefits from dehydrating this way. First, it cuts the dehydration time down quite a bit, using less energy, which is better for our planet. Second, it helps prevent bacteria growth and fermentation that can occur when you dehydrate at lower temperatures for longer periods of time.

It is a good idea to rotate your shelves when you are dehydrating. You can rotate them from front to back and from top to bottom. The back and the top of the dehydrators are the warmest places.

I also calibrate my dehydrators. An oven thermometer works well for this. Place it on the top shelf and let it run long enough to get an accurate temperature.

Times are estimates. Different dehydrators will dry at different speeds. Air humidity can even affect drying times. The best way to deal with this is to keep an eye on your food as it dehydrates.

There are certain foods that you are going to want to dehydrate completely dry, such as crackers and flat breads. Others should be somewhat chewy. The recipes give you suggested times and textures.

Ingredients: Always make sure you are using the freshest ingredients when making your raw recipes. Fruit should be ripe, but not overly ripe. Vegetables should be fresh and used as close to purchasing as possible. We don't have the option of cooking to cover up not-so-great ingredients. So, do yourself a big favor and use the best possible that you can get.

Frozen Vegetables and Fruits: I often get asked about frozen vegetables and fruits. If you can't get fresh, frozen can work in a pinch. I opt for organic. Vegetables and fruits that are flash frozen on the spot, directly after picking, often have more nutrients than fresh produce that has been picked too early and shipped thousands of miles.

Raw Oats and Raw Oat Flour: See the ingredient list on page 240 for more information on these products.

Storing Raw Food: I often get asked how long recipes keep. Honestly, just use common sense. If it is something that has been dehydrated completely dry (like flatbreads), it will last much longer than something that still has moisture in it. Everything else? It's raw, fresh food. Treat it as such.

Storage Containers: With all the information on plastics leaching chemicals into our foods, I prefer to use glass containers to store food. They work great in the refrigerator and freezer. They do have plastic tops, but if your food isn't touching, you should be OK.

Soaking Nuts: You will notice that many of the recipes call for nuts and seeds to be soaked overnight. There are two reasons for this. First, nuts and seeds contain enzyme inhibitors that make them harder to digest. When soaked overnight, these enzyme inhibitors are deactivated, allowing for easier digestion. Second, many of the recipes call for nuts to be soaked for textural reasons. Cashews will blend more smoothly when presoaked. You can read more about soaking nuts on page xviii.

Sprouting Grains and Seeds: Sprouted grains and seeds are super-nutrition-packed powerhouse jewels. When you sprout grains, their life force is activated. You are literally taking a dry grain and turning it into a living, growing plant. When the growth cycle is activated, all kinds of wonderful things happen. Vitamin C and Vitamin B increase. Carotene increases while phytic acid (a substance we don't want) gets neutralized. Sprouting concentrates the the nutrients and also makes the grains easier to digest. And even the enzymes that we love so much are increased during sprouting.

Sprouting is easy: Put a cup or two (what ever the recipe calls for) of the grain into a jar, fill with water, and let soak overnight. In the morning, pour off the water and rinse two to three times a day until you see a little tail starting to grow. At this point, you can dehydrate the grains and grind them into sprouted flour or use them as is.

Sprouted seeds can be added to salads, wraps, and many other dishes for taste, nutrients, and a little added crunch.

Substitutions: There isn't a day that goes by that I don't get a request for substitutions. Nuts, flax, avocado, young Thai coconut, grains, etc., all seem to be things that people have issues with. Substitution requests are frustrating because it isn't as simple as one would think.

When I create a recipe, great care is taken when combining ingredients. I am looking for a balance between the flavors, textures, and of course, visual appeal. How the ingredients interact with each other is also very important. Changing one ingredient can affect how the recipe comes together.

Balance is very important because without it, your food won't be appealing. That said, feel free to experiment. Taste as you go and be aware of the role the ingredient that you are replacing plays. If it is the backbone of the recipe, be cautious. But when substituting things that are very similar (raisins for craisins), go for it and have fun!

Buying Seasonally: It is always a good idea to try to make recipes with ingredients that are in season. You will save money and also get the freshest produce available. You can also freeze many fruits and veggies. Just know that the texture may change. Example: I freeze a lot of zucchini, but only in pureed form.

Maple Syrup: It is not raw but is frequently used in raw food recipes.

Ingredients: There is a list of the more uncommon ingredients plus where to order them on page 240.

Raw Food Pantry

When you first start on your journey with raw food, it can be intimidating. I often hear people say, "I could never eat a raw food diet; it is too time-consuming and difficult." In reality, when your pantry and refrigerator are set up properly, you will find yourself spending less time preparing food and more time enjoying it. With just a little forethought, raw food can be delicious, quick, and satisfying.

"How long will this keep?" is a question that I get constantly. The most important thing to remember is that you are simply working with uncooked food, and common sense should apply. The same rules apply to raw recipes that apply to storing produce, grains, and nuts. That said, there are a few things that you will want to keep in mind.

Nuts: I like to have a complete stock of nuts on hand at all times (see list). I store all of my nuts in the refrigerator or freezer. Nuts have oils and can go rancid if stored at room temperature. I buy my nuts in bulk either at my local co-op or online. Many times you can get a better price online and also get a fresher product.

You also will want to presoak some of your nuts before using. Nuts contain enzyme inhibitors that can interfere with digestion. To understand this, think about a nut that is waiting to grow. It sits dormant (enzyme inhibitors) until it is introduced to the proper environment (moisture). If you soak your nuts in water for 6–12 hours, the enzyme inhibitors dissipate and healthy enzymes become more active as the nut starts to come alive as the sprouting process is activated.

I usually soak and dehydrate my nuts and seeds as soon as I get them home. That way, they will be ready for use. A point of clarification: If a recipe calls for 1 cup cashews, soaked at least 6 hours, you need to resoak the seeds for that recipe as it is involving a textural element and added water. A side benefit to soaking nuts (and seeds) is that they taste better.

Nuts will keep for weeks when refrigerated and months when frozen. Recipes made from nuts will have a much shorter time frame. I normally only plan on 2–3 days for nutmilks, desserts, and sauces that are made from nuts. Many of the sauces that are nut based can be frozen.

Dried Grains and Beans: I keep a good selection of grains and beans to sprout on hand. They keep for months in a dark, cool place. My preferred storage containers are glass as there will be no chemical reaction between the glass and the food. You still want to make sure you are getting the freshest food, so it is a good idea to not buy more than you will use in a few months.

Fresh Produce: The backbone of the raw food diet is fresh produce, so you want to get your produce as fresh as possible. In the summer months, I love frequenting the farmer's markets. I know that everything I am buying was most likely picked that morning. Every minute that passes from picking to table degrades our food a bit. Frozen produce can work in a pinch and sometimes has even higher nutrients than fresh, if the fresh has traveled a long way. Today's methods of freezing do not require parboiling. They flash freeze right as the food comes out of the field.

If you are able to grow your own produce, that is even better. Not only do you get the great satisfaction of eating something you grew, it is the freshest food available.

Make sure you are using your produce at its peak. The taste of your ingredients will dramatically affect the final dish. Start with a poor-tasting apple and you will get a poor-tasting apple pie. This effect multiplies with raw food. This effect increases when you are not using the masking techniques of cooking. What you start with is what you will end up with.

A quick tip about fresh produce: If you have produce that you know you are not going to get to before it starts to go bad, throw it in the freezer. Even lettuce and spinach can be frozen and used later in green drinks and smoothies. I am often slicing up bananas and throwing them in the freezer just before they go bad. It is a great way to avoid waste.

Ordering Online: Many of the products that I use regularly, such as coconut oil, coconut butter, cacao powder, chia seeds, etc., can be found at much better prices online. Take some time to compare prices. Use your Google-fu and do the research. You will be paying a little shipping, but when comparing to the higher prices you will find locally and also the time you will save, it is worth the effort. Your products will be delivered right to your door, fresh and ready to use, oftentimes at a significant savings.

Storing Food in the Refrigerator: The rule of thumb? Use the same guidelines that you would for fresh produce. If your food has had a trip to the dehydrator, it will stay fresh a little longer. Just keep an eye on it for changes. If the smell changes, or the look changes, it is a great indicator that the food isn't fresh anymore. You can even get a little more shelf life from your dehydrated recipes when you store them in the refrigerator. Just make sure they are in an airtight container, as you don't want to introduce moisture to food you have dehydrated.

With a little planning, you can set up a great pantry with the basics that will allow you to create great raw food meals. The Pantry List on the next page is what I often work off of.

Pantry List

Nuts:
Almonds
Cashews
Walnuts
Macadamia Nuts
Brazil Nuts
Pine Nuts
Pecans

Seeds:
Flax Seeds
Sunflower Seeds
Hemp Seeds
Pumpkin Seeds
Chia Seeds
Sesame Seeds

Grains:
Wheat Berries
Buckwheat
Kamut
Quinoa
Chickpeas

Fruit:
Grapes
Apples
Lemons
Oranges
Limes
Strawberries
Blueberries
Bananas
Young Thai Coconut

Veggies:
Greens
Spinach
Kale
Tomatoes
Cucumber
Zucchini
Celery
Beets
Jicama
Carrots
Cabbage
Onions
Garlic
Parsley
Avocado

Dried Fruit:
Cranberries
Raisins
Dates

Other:
Coconut Oil
Coconut Butter
Himalayan Salt
Honey
Agave Nectar
Nama Shoyu
Nutritional Yeast*
Maple Syrup*
Cacao Powder

*Not raw but used frequently in raw recipes.

drinks

Good Morning Green Drink

2 cups spinach
1 ½ cups grapes
2 carrots
½ cucumber
½-inch piece of ginger
1 stalk celery
2 dates
handful ice
½ to 1 cup water

1. Combine all ingredients in a high-speed blender. Start with ½ cup water and add more to desired thickness.
2. Blend until smooth.

Almond Milk

MAKES 4 CUPS

1 cup almonds, soaked overnight, rinsed, and drained
4 cups water

1. Place almonds and water in high-speed blender. Blend for 3-5 minutes.
2. Pour almond-water mixture into nut-milk bag or layers of cheesecloth. Squeeze the bag until all of the "milk" is in bowl and only the nut pulp remains in the bag.

Sweet Almond Milk

MAKES 4 CUPS

1 cup almonds, soaked overnight, rinsed, and drained
4 cups filtered water
2 dates
1 vanilla bean

1. Place all ingredients in high-speed blender.
2. Process for 2 minutes.
3. Strain through nut-milk bag.

*Chef's Note: You can save the remaining pulp, dehydrate it, and use it as flour for other recipes.

Hazelnut Milk

MAKES 3 CUPS

1 cup hazelnuts, soaked overnight, rinsed, and drained
3 cups water

1.   Place hazelnuts and water in high-speed blender.
2.   Blend for 2 minutes.
3.   Strain through nut-milk bag.

Brazil Nut Milk

MAKES 3 CUPS

1 cup Brazil nuts
3 cups water

1.   Follow instructions for hazelnut milk above.

Rejuvelac

1 cup rinsed wheat berries

Sprouted Wheat Berries

1. Place rinsed wheat berries in a sprouting jar. Cover with water and let sit for 24 hours.
2. Drain water.
3. Rinse 3–4 times a day until small tails sprout.

Rejuvelac

½ cup sprouted wheat berries (sprouted just until tails start)
4 cups water

1. Place the wheat berries and the water in a jar.
2. Leave in a warm place for 24–48 hours. You will see a little fizz. The liquid should be a little tart but not smell.

Blueberry Grape Drink

SERVES 2

3 cups romaine lettuce
1 cup spinach
1 ½ cups grapes
1 cup blueberries
½ to 1 cup filtered water

1. Place in high-speed blender, blend, and drink!

Warm Cacao with Cinnamon

2 cups sweetened almond milk (see page 4)
1–2 tablespoons cacao powder, to taste
1 tablespoon agave nectar, or more to taste
sprinkle of cinnamon

1. Combine all ingredients in a blender or with an immersion blender. The blender will thicken it nicely.
2. Warm to 115 degrees. You can do this in a high-speed blender or VERY carefully on the stove. If you use the stove, you need to stop heating before it gets to temp as it will continue to heat even after the heat source is removed. You can use a candy thermometer to check temp.

Pineapple Grape Green Drink

SERVES 2

3 cups spinach
1 cup grapes
1 cup pineapple
½ cup filtered water

1. Place all ingredients in high-speed blender, blend, and drink!

Cacao Banana Pick-Me-Up

SERVES 1

1 cup Brazil Nut Milk (see page 5)
1 cup ice
1 banana
1 tablespoon raw honey or agave nectar
2 tablespoons cacao powder

1. Place all ingredients in blender, blend until smooth.

Warm Hazelnut Cinnamon Milk

SERVES 2

2 cups Hazelnut Milk (see page 5)
1 tablespoon raw honey (can add more if you like it sweeter)
½ teaspoon cinnamon

1. Mix all ingredients together, warm in dehydrator or over double boiler.
2. You can use a kitchen thermometer to make sure you keep the temp under 115 degrees for raw.

"Eggless" Nog

½ cup almonds
1 young Thai coconut, flesh from
3 dates
3 tablespoons agave nectar
1 ½ teaspoon cinnamon
½ teaspoons nutmeg
½ teaspoon cloves
½ teaspoon rum extract (not raw but completes the
eggnog flavor)
3 cups water

1. Place all ingredients in blender and blend until very smooth.
2. Strain through nut-milk bag.
3. Top with a sprinkle of extra nutmeg. You can serve this warm
   or cold.

Watermelon Lemonade

SERVES 2

4 cups watermelon
2 lemons, juice from
agave nectar, to taste

1. Blend watermelon and lemon juice in blender.
2. Add agave to taste.

breakfast

Raw Cinnamon Buns

$\mathcal{I}$ have come across a couple of raw cinnamon bun recipes, but none seemed close enough to traditional cinnamon buns. What a great challenge. Almond flour, flaked spelt (yup, you heard me right!), and ground flax are the perfect medium for these. A bit of time in the dehydrator provides the perfect consistency. To get away from only using cashews for cream fillings, I also add almonds and raisins. The crowning glory is the maple cashew icing! I wouldn't suggest these for breakfast every morning, but for a Sunday brunch or a weekend treat they are perfect.

Spelt is a grain that is related to wheat, but contains much more protein and fewer carbohydrates. It is high in B vitamins, iron, and potassium. You can replace it with raw, flaked oats if you wish, but you know me—I like to mix it up a bit!

Buns

MAKES 12

5 dates
¼ cup water
1 cup flax seeds, ground
1 ¼ cups almond flour
1 cup spelt flakes
1 cup pecans, chopped fine
2 teaspoons cinnamon
3 tablespoons olive oil
¼ cup agave nectar
1 cup water

1. Soak dates until soft. Blend with ¼ cup water to make a smooth date paste. Set aside.

Continued…

Buns continued...

2. Combine flax, almond flour (I use the dehydrated almond pulp left over from making almond milk), finely chopped pecans, and spelt flakes.
3. In a separate bowl, combine date paste, olive oil, agave, and water.
4. Mix wet ingredients into dry. Spread in a rectangle on a non-stick dehydrator sheet. You want this to be a little less than ½ inch thick.
5. Dehydrate for 30 minutes. Flip onto screen, peel off dehydrator sheet, and dehydrate for another 20 minutes.

*Chef's Note: While the bun is dehydrating, you will want to prepare the filling.

Filling

1 young Thai coconut, flesh from
1 cup cashews, soaked overnight, rinsed, and drained
½ cup almonds, soaked overnight, rinsed, and drained
¼ cup agave nectar
1 tablespoon vanilla
½ cup raisins

1. Place all ingredients except raisins in food processor, process until smooth.
2. Stir in raisins.

Assembly

1. Place "bun" on parchment paper.
2. Spread filling on bun. You can spread to the edges on the long sides but leave an inch or two on the short sides.
3. Gently roll up.
4. Slice and top with icing.

Banana Pecan Pancakes

When I was a little girl, every Sunday after church my family would go to our local pancake restaurant. I still have those Sunday morning pancake cravings but no desire to eat traditional pancakes. For Mother's Day, I created a raw food recipe for my favorite pancakes, banana pecan! They are amazingly filling, and will satisfy the desire for a special Sunday morning breakfast.

MAKES 4–6 PANCAKES

1 ½ cups flax seeds, ground
½ cup flax seeds
½ cup dried coconut, unsweetened
¾ cup water
¼ cup agave nectar or maple syrup
¼ cup coconut butter, softened
1 cup bananas, sliced
¾ cup chopped pecans

1. Mix all ingredients together. You might want to use your hands as the batter is stiff.
2. Shape into pancake-sized patties.
3. Place on dehydrator shelf with screen. Dehydrate at 140 degrees for 30 minutes, then 116 degrees for another 30 minutes. These should still be moist.

Raw Strawberry Banana Crepes

Before I started eating raw, my girls and I had a Sunday tradition: We made Swedish pancakes. Butter, cream, whipped cream, white flour, and lots of sugar. Maybe a little dollop of strawberries. They tasted great but guaranteed a food coma plus a day of feeling heavy and bloated. I traded an energized, productive day for a few minutes of culinary gluttony.

My body no longer tolerates white flour, sugar, and cream—not to mention the potential for damage caused from eating that way! Still, I miss that Sunday tradition. I created a raw version of that special Sunday breakfast to fill the void. Be sure to start the crepes the night before.

Crepes

MAKES 4

4 bananas
1 lemon, juice from

1. Place bananas in food processor. Add lemon juice and process until liquid.
2. Pour into 5-inch rounds. These should only be about ⅛ inch thick, so spread mixture if necessary.
3. Dehydrate overnight at 110 degrees. Do not overdry these. I start them just before I go to bed. You want them to be flexible.

Cashew Vanilla Cream

2 young Thai coconuts, flesh from (about 1 ½ cups)
1 cup cashews, soaked overnight
splash of Madagascar vanilla
1 tablespoon agave nectar (optional)

1. Place the cashews in high-speed blender. Blend on high speed.
2. Add the coconut meat and vanilla. Process until well blended. Refrigerate to thicken, if needed.

Assembly

assorted berries

1. Spoon the Cashew Vanilla Cream into half the crepe. Top with berries and add more cream. Fold over and experience joy!

Blueberry Flax Pancakes

MAKES 5 FIVE-INCH PANCAKES
THESE ARE VERY FILLING!

½ cup flax seeds, ground
1 cup flax seeds, whole
3 tablespoons coconut oil, melted
¼ cup agave nectar
½ cup water
1 cup blueberries
¼ coconut, unsweetened, dried

1. Mix all ingredients.
2. Dehydrate at 145 degrees for 1 hour, flip, and then dehydrate
    for 30 minutes at 115 degrees.

Doughnut Holes

$\mathcal{W}$hen I first started experimenting with raw food, I came across a raw food recipe for "doughnut holes." Wanting something that reminded me of a cinnamon doughnut hole, I threw together this recipe. Made with Brazil nuts for a base, some raw oat flour, flaked oats, and coconut oil, a quick roll in cinnamon and Sucanat makes these a great-tasting treat.

Brazil nuts are nutrient dense. They are full of protein, copper, niacin, magnesium, fiber, vitamin E, and selenium. Selenium is a powerful antioxidant that helps neutralize dangerous free radicals. Sucanat is an unrefined sugar cane juice. It is made by heating, so is not considered raw but, like maple syrup, is not processed.

MAKES 2 DOZEN

2 cups Brazil nuts
½ cup raw oat flour
1 cup raw flaked oats
⅓ cup coconut oil
⅓ cup maple syrup

1. Chop Brazil nuts in food processor until fine.
2. Combine dry ingredients in a bowl.
3. Combine wet ingredients, mix together, and then add to the wet ingredients. Stir.
4. Squeeze into balls. Roll in topping mixture and refrigerate.

Topping

⅓ cup Sucanat
1 ½ teaspoons cinnamon

1. Combine Sucanat and cinnamon.
2. Blend. I use a coffee grinder for this to break up the grainy Sucanat. You can skip this step and just combine the ingredients.

Flaked Oats with Goji Berries

*I*n the winter, I find myself wanting more than a green drink for breakfast. The perfect solution? Flaked oats! High in soluble and insoluble fiber, oats are known to reduce blood cholesterol. They can also help regulate blood sugar, aid in digestion, and, because they contain phytochemicals, they help reduce the risk of cancer. Studies have also shown that they help control blood pressure and are an excellent source of energy-giving carbohydrates.

Since I found organic, flaked oats I can use raw, I have put oatmeal back on the breakfast menu! This takes a little advanced preparation, and you will be using the dehydrator, so plan accordingly. I normally make them right when I get up. Then they will be ready when you are done showering!

MAKES 1 SERVING

1 cup raw flaked oats
½ to 1 cup almond milk
¼ cup goji berries
¼ cup chopped almonds
agave nectar or maple syrup, to taste

1. Place oats in glass bowl. Cover with almond milk.
2. Stir in goji berries. Place in dehydrator at 145 degrees for 30 minutes, reduce temp, and continue for another 30 minutes. You can also start soaking the oats the night before and then gently warm in the dehydrator.
3. Top with walnuts and sweeten to taste.

Cinnamon Raisin "Toast" and Hazelnut Butter

When I wake to a dark and chilly house, my green drink is not enough to satisfy me. I have been working on a raw food recipe for a breakfast "toast" and finally came up with one I love.

This "toast" is made with sunflower seeds, almonds, carrots, and apples spiked with cinnamon and raisins. My recreation of Cinnamon Raisin Toast. Healthy, hearty and tasty, you will love this raw start to your morning!

Toast

MAKES APPROXIMATELY 2 SHEETS

2 cups almonds
1 cup sunflower seeds
1 cup flax seeds, ground
1 cup zucchini, pureed
2 carrots
1 apple
1 cup raisins
4 dates + ½ cup water
1 teaspoon cinnamon

1. Place sunflower seeds in food processor and process until finely chopped. Place in bowl.
2. Place almonds in food processor and finely chop. Place in bowl with sunflower seeds.
3. Add flax and stir to combine.
4. Process carrots and apple in food processor until you get a puree. Add zucchini puree, mix.
5. In blender, blend dates with ½ cup water until liquefied. You can soak the dates first to soften.

6. Add to carrot and apple mixture and stir.
7. Stir wet ingredients into dry. Mix well.
8. Stir in cinnamon and raisins.
9. Spread ¼ inch thick on nonstick dehydrator tray. Dehydrate for 1 hour at 145 degrees, reduce heat and continue to dehydrate at 116 degrees for 2 more hours.
10. Flip mixture onto screen, peel off nonstick sheet, and continue to dehydrate for about 4–6 more hours or until dry but not hard. This bread should be a little soft. Top with Hazelnut Butter.

Hazelnut Butter

2 cups hazelnuts
2 tablespoons olive oil

1. Place ingredients in food processor.
2. Process until paste forms, scraping sides frequently. This will take some time.

appetizers

Sun-Dried Tomato Pumpkin Seed Pesto

MAKES 6 SERVINGS

2 cloves garlic
1 cup pumpkin seeds
¼ cup olive oil
1 teaspoon lemon juice
pinch Himalayan salt (optional)
½ cup basil, coarsely chopped
⅓ cup sun-dried tomatoes, coarsely chopped

1. With food processor running, drop in cloves of garlic. Let process until garlic is chopped. Scrape down sides of the processor.
2. Add pumpkin seeds, olive oil, lemon juice, and salt. Process until very well combined and you have a pesto consistency.
3. Add chopped basil. Process until well combined.
4. Add sun-dried tomatoes and process until combined.

Pine Nut Parmesan

½ cup pine nuts
pinch Himalayan salt

1. Process pine nuts and salt in food processor until a coarse meal is achieved.

Basil Sun-Dried Tomato Spread

1 cup Basil Walnut-Cashew Spread (*see below*)
¼ cup sun-dried tomatoes, chopped

1. Stir sun-dried tomatoes into spread. Use as a dip, or a topping on crackers or veggies.

Basil Walnut-Cashew Spread

2 cups cashews, soaked for 6 hours and drained
½ cup walnuts, soaked for 6 hours and drained
½ cup filtered water
2 tablespoons basil oil (*see below*)
2 cloves garlic
1 teaspoon lemon juice
pinch Himalayan salt
pinch ground pepper

1. Place all ingredients in food processor. Process until well blended.

Basil Oil

2 cups packed basil
1 cup cold-pressed olive oil

1. Place basil and oil in blender.
2. Blend until well combined.
3. Strain. This will keep in the refrigerator for a couple of weeks.

Honey Balsamic

2 tablespoons raw honey or agave
¼ cup balsamic vinegar

1. Add raw honey (or agave) to balsamic vinegar.
2. Whisk.

Appetizer: Tomatoes with Sun-Dried Tomato Pumpkin Seed Pesto

2 tomatoes
basil leaves

1. Place 1 slice of tomato on plate. Top with pesto. Sprinkle Pine
   Nut Parmesan on top. Sprinkle with Honey Balsamic Vinegar.
   Place basil leaf and sun dried-tomato for garnish.

This pesto can also be utilized as a main course.

Baba Ghanoush

I have always loved eggplant, especially in Baba Ghanoush (eggplant and garlic dip). I wanted a raw version, but raw eggplant can be bitter and have an unpleasant texture. I discovered if you dice and freeze it, once thawed, it can achieve the texture you need. This also eliminates some of the bitterness associated with raw eggplant.

Nutritionally, eggplant contains chlorogenic acid, which is one of the most potent free-radical scavengers found in plants. Benefits attributed to chlorogenic acid include antimutagenic (anticancer), antimicrobial, anti-LDL (bad cholesterol), and antiviral activities. It is also very high in fiber.

This recipe is full of raw garlic, which I love and feel is the best thing about it! However, you might want to add it slowly to suit your taste.

MAKES ABOUT 2 CUPS

2–3 cloves garlic
½ cup cashews, soaked for at least 6 hours
1 large eggplant, diced, frozen, and thawed
¼ cup tahini
½ lemon, juice from
2 tablespoons olive oil
pinch Himalayan salt

1. Start food processor and drop garlic, clove by clove, into the spinning blade. It will fine dice it and throw it on the wall of the processor.
2. Add the cashews and process until smooth.
3. Add diced eggplant, tahini, lemon juice, olive oil and pinch of salt. Process until smooth.

Enjoy with your choice of flatbreads.

Corn Flax Chips and Guacamole

*O*ne of my favorite after-work treats has always been chips and guacamole. Trying to be more healthy, I switched to blue corn chips with flax. Though a little healthier, they're still full of salt, with the nutrients baked right out of them. More empty calories. So, the challenge was to create a raw food recipe for chips that worked with my chunky guacamole and satisfied my salty, crunchy tooth. The answer is raw corn chips! Combined with a fast-to-assemble, chunky guacamole, this is a perfect dish for snacking, entertaining, or even a meal!

Corn Chips

MAKES ONE SHEET. THIS RECIPE CAN EASILY BE DOUBLED.

3 cups corn, fresh or frozen
¼ onion
1 teaspoon smoked paprika
½ teaspoon cayenne
1–2 pinches Himalayan salt

1. Place all ingredients in a food processor and blend until smooth.
2. Spread on a nonstick sheet on dehydrator tray. Score the mixture before you start to dehydrate.
3. Dehydrate at 140 degrees for 30 minutes, reduce heat to 115 degrees and dehydrate for 12 hours.
4. Flip crackers and dehydrate until fully dry. Break apart at score lines.

Continued...

Guacamole

MAKES 2 CUPS

2 avocados, mashed
1 medium purple onion, diced
1 tomato, diced
1 lime, juice from
½ small, finely diced hot pepper
pinch of Himalayan salt

1. Mix ingredients together.
2. Serve and enjoy.

Kale Chips

*F*or all versions: Wash kale and spin dry. Remove the tough spine and tear into bite-size pieces, keeping in mind that they will shrink in size as they dehydrate.

Version One

3 tablespoons olive oil
1 teaspoon Himalayan salt

1. Combine olive oil and sea salt in large bowl. Stir in kale and coat.
2. Place on dehydrator sheets and dehydrate at 115 degrees for 4–6 hours or until crisp.

Version Two

3 tablespoons olive oil
2 cloves garlic
1 teaspoon thyme

1. With food processor running, drop garlic in. It will mince. Add oil and thyme.
2. Place mixture in bowl and follow directions above.

Continued...

Kale Chips continued...

Version Three

1 clove garlic
1 cup cashews, soaked overnight, rinsed, and drained
¼ cup nutritional yeast
⅓ cup water
2 tablespoons olive oil
½ teaspoon smoked paprika
¼ teaspoon chipotle (spice)
pinch Himalayan salt

1.   With processor running, drop in garlic and mince.
2.   Add the rest of the ingredients and process until smooth.
3.   Pour over kale chips in a bowl and massage until kale is coated.
4.   Dehydrate on screens at 115 degrees for 4–6 hours or until crisp.

*Chef's Note: Since creating these recipes, I have found that if you roughly chop the kale into 1-inch pieces, the whole process goes much faster! You can just spread the pieces on the dehydrator sheet, it doesn't matter if they are touching a little.

Pea Pods with Sun-Dried Tomato Spread

Sun-dried tomatoes are a favorite around here. Something magical happens when you condense the flavors through drying. I had sun-dried tomatoes on the brain one day when I started working on some raw food recipes. Wanting something quick and versatile, I came up with a little spread that could double as a "pasta" sauce. I love anything that will cut down on my time in the kitchen!

MAKES 1–2 CUPS

1 cup cashews, soaked overnight, rinsed, and drained
½ cup pine nuts, soaked until soft
¼ cup sun-dried tomatoes, softened
½ lemon, juice from
½ shallot, about 2 tablespoons
1 clove garlic
pinch Himalayan salt
1 cup fresh pea pods, split

1. Combine cashews and pine nuts with the rest of the ingredients in food processor and process until smooth.
3. Pipe into split pea pods.

*Chef's Note: You will have left over spread. It will keep in the refrigerator for at least 3–4 days. You can use this for the pasta recipe on page 149.

Zucchini "Fries"

2 medium zucchinis
1 clove garlic
3 tablespoons olive oil
pinch Himalayan salt
pinch pepper
2 tablespoons nutritional yeast (optional)

1. Cut zucchini into pieces. These should be about ½ x ½ x 4 inches. They dehydrate quite a bit, so don't be afraid to make them big enough.
2. Put garlic through press.
3. Combine garlic, oil, salt, and pepper. Put in large bowl and add nutritional yeast (optional).
4. Toss to coat zucchini.
5. Place on screens and dehydrate at 140 degrees for 30 minutes, reduce heat to 115 degrees, and continue to dehydrate for 4–5 hours.

Pepper Poppers with Pine Nut Filling and "Bacon"

*T*his recipe was inspired by a raw food pot luck I hosted. Talking to people at all levels of involvement with raw food was interesting and enlightening. It is always fun to see what raw food dishes people show up with. One couple brought some jalapeno poppers, made the raw food way. In my version, I opted for small red cayenne peppers, for the color and the ripeness. The heat is about the same. The filling is made from pine nuts, cashews, and a few other ingredients. Eggplant "bacon" tops complete the bite-size morsels. There are quite a few recipes out there for eggplant "bacon." This one was inspired by a trip to the spice shop and a desire to make it quick and easy. It turned out great. I had to fight my daughter to keep enough for the photos!

The day before, make the bacon.

Eggplant Bacon

MAKES 2 DOZEN

1 eggplant
2 tablespoons olive oil
¼ cup water
1 teaspoon smoked paprika
½ teaspoon ground chipotle peppers (I get them preground)
2 tablespoons agave nectar

1. Using a vegetable peeler or mandolin, slice the eggplant into strips about ⅛ inch thick. Set aside.
2. Mix together marinade ingredients.
3. Place eggplant in marinade, making sure all is covered, and let soak for 5–6 hours.
4. Dehydrate at 116 degrees for at least 12 hours, or until crisp.

Pine Nut Filling

1 ½ cups pine nuts, soaked for 6+ hours and drained
½ cup cashews, soaked overnight, rinsed, and drained
1 ½ lemons, juice from
¼ cup water
2 tablespoons nutritional yeast
1 tablespoon smoked paprika
pinch Himalayan salt
½ red pepper

1. Place all ingredients in food processor and process until smooth.

Assembly

10 cayenne peppers
Filling
Eggplant Bacon

1. Cut peppers in half and remove seeds and white membranes. I use plastic gloves when doing this, be careful to not touch your face.
2. Fill pepper halves with pine nut cheese and top with eggplant bacon. Enjoy!

Cashew Cheese

*N*ut cheeses are a great item to have in your repertoire. They are tasty, easily support the addition of many herbs and spices, and will impress your raw and non-raw friends alike! It can seem a bit daunting, but a few handfuls of cashews, some Rejuvelac, and a little patience turns out a delightful cheese spread that is a welcome addition to any raw diet.

In case you are wondering what rejuvelac is, it is a fermented liquid made from sprouting wheat berries that is said to be high in enzymes, friendly bacteria, vitamins and minerals.

MAKES A 2-CUP ROUND

2 cups cashews
½ cups Rejuvelac (see page 6)
Himalayan salt (optional)

1. Cover cashews with water and soak overnight. Drain off water.
2. Place cashews in high-speed blender and process with Rejuvelac until a smooth paste forms. You can add a dash of Himalayan salt.
3. Line a strainer with 2 layers of cheese cloth. Spoon mixture into the cloth.
4. Set in a warm place and let set for 24 hours. Form into the shape you want. I coated the outside with cracked pepper. Put in refrigerator to finish setting.

Rawchos

Sun-dried Tomato Cashew Cheese Spread (see page 60)
Corn Flax Chips (see page 59)
Mock Sour Cream (see page 59)
1 avocado, cubed
1 tomato, cubed

1. Layer Corn Flax Chips on plate.
2. Crumble Sun-dried Tomato Cashew Cheese Spread on top of chips.
3. Top with chopped avocado, tomatoes, and Mock Sour Cream.

Turmeric Veggie Dip

MAKES 2 CUPS

1 cup cashews, soaked overnight and drained
1 cup young coconut flesh, about 1–2 young Thai coconuts
¼ coconut water, from young coconut
2 tablespoons olive oil
1 clove garlic
2 teaspoons turmeric
1 teaspoon ginger
2 tablespoons agave nectar
1 sliced cucumber
other dipping veggies (celery, carrots, etc.), (optional)

1. Place all ingredients in food processor and process until smooth. This will take a bit and you will need to stop and scrape down the sides occasionally.
2. Slice cucumber and pipe the dip onto rounds.
3. Alternatively, cut up veggies and use as a dip. (I sprinkled a little paprika on top for the photo.)

Onion Rings

I love converting unhealthy recipes to healthy, raw food recipes. Onion rings were always one of my favorite treats, but I refuse to eat the deep-fried variety anymore. They are soaked with oil and breaded with nothing health promoting. I still love them and wanted to find a healthy way to enjoy them.

I have seen a few onion ring recipes, but I wanted something that was similar to the traditional way of making them. Choosing the technique of soaking the onions, I employed almond milk. You will use the almond milk for soaking and also for breading the rings. Once you make the milk, save the nut pulp, dehydrate it, and combine it with spices and a little flax. One warning… you really need to use a mild or sweet onion for this recipe or the onion flavor will be too strong.

Almond Milk

1 cup almonds, soaked over night, rinsed, and drained
4 cups water

1. Combine soaked almonds and water in blender.
2. Strain through nut-milk bag. Save the pulp and dehydrate it.

Onion Rings

1 *large sweet onion*
4 *cups almond milk*
¾ *cup almond milk pulp, dehydrated*
1 *cup ground flax seeds, ground*
1 *tablespoon smoked paprika*
½ *teaspoon ground chipotle*
½ *teaspoon Himalayan salt*

1. Slice onions and place in zip lock bag with almond milk. Soak while pulp is dehydrating.
2. When pulp is done dehydrating, place in food processor with flax, spices, and salt.
3. Separate into 2 batches. If you use all of it at once, a lot of it will become saturated and too wet to use. Splitting it into separate batches protects against waste.
4. Drain onion rings, reserving milk. Dip onion ring in the milk, then in the almond-flax mixture, dip in milk once again, and then in almond-flax mixture again to get a heavier coating.
5. Dehydrate at 115 degrees for 6–8 hours until almost dry. You want the onions to retain a little moisture, the breading should be dry.

Sweet Potato Fries with Chipotle "Mayo"

Eating a raw food diet doesn't mean giving up some of your favorite foods. I used to love to order sweet potato fries with chipotle mayo. But my body did not love eating them! I felt heavy, bloated, and like I had been sedated! The deep frying plus all the saturated fat in the mayo completely obliterated any healthy benefits that the sweet potatoes were offering. The potatoes offered in this raw food recipe are a little more chewy than crispy but still great! And the "mayo" is even better than the original unhealthy version!

Sweet potatoes are a nutritional power house. High in vitamin A and vitamin C, they are also loaded with fiber. They are excellent immunity builders and also help balance blood sugars. Adding these wonderful tubers to your diet provides a great healthy way to snack.

3 large sweet potatoes
½ cup Nama Shoyu
½ cup olive oil

1. Slice sweet potatoes into fry shapes. These will dehydrate down quite a bit, so I usually start with about ⅓ inch x ⅓ inch.
2. Mix together Nama Shoyu and olive oil. Pour into a large zip lock bag and add sweet potatoes. (You can also use any type container, just make sure that the potato slices are covered).
3. Marinate over night. Drain, place on dehydrator screens, sprinkle with sea salt, and dehydrate at 145 degrees for 30 minutes. Reduce temp to 115 degrees and dehydrate until desired dryness is achieved.
4. You will want to check them after about 4 hours. Some people like them very dry, I tend to like them less dehydrated.

Continued...

Sweet Potato Fries with Chipotle "Mayo" continued...

Chipotle "Mayo"

1 cup pine nuts, soaked for 3 hours
2 tablespoons olive oil
1 lemon, juice from
½ to 1 clove garlic
¼ cup filtered water
½ cup young Thai coconut flesh
3 teaspoons chipotle seasoning

1. Place all ingredients in high-speed blender and blend until
    very smooth.

Corn Flax Chips

6 cups corn, fresh or frozen and thawed
1 red pepper
2 limes, juice from
2 cloves garlic
1 teaspoon cayenne
1 teaspoon paprika
1 cup flax seeds, ground

1. Combine all ingredients except ground flax in food processor and pulse until well combined.
2. Remove from processor and stir in the flax seeds.
3. Spread onto nonstick sheets and score lightly. This batter is sticky, so you may have to wet your hands when spreading it out.
4. Dehydrate at 145 degrees for 1 hour, then 115 degrees for 5–6 hours. Flip chips over, remove nonstick sheets and finish dehydrating until dry.

Mock Sour Cream

1 young Thai coconut, flesh from
¼ cup soaked cashews, soaked overnight, rinsed, and drained
½ lemon, juice from
½ lime, juice from
1 tablespoon white miso
½ cup water

1. Combine all ingredients in a high-speed blender. Blend until smooth.

Sun-Dried Tomato Cashew Cheese Spread

1 cup cashews, soaked overnight, rinsed, and drained
½ shallot, coarsely chopped
1 lemon, juice from
1 clove garlic
pinch Himalayan salt
½ cup smoked sun-dried tomatoes, chopped

1. Turn on food processor and while blade is running, drop the clove of garlic in.
2. Once it is chopped, add the cashews, shallot, lemon juice, and pinch of sea salt. Process until a thick paste forms.
3. Add chopped sun-dried tomatoes and process until tomatoes are incorporated into the mixture. There will still be some chunks of tomato.

Cheese Spread Three Ways

MAKES ONE 1 OF EACH SPREAD

The Base

3 cups cashews, soaked overnight, rinsed, and drained
1 cup pine nuts
1 lemon, juice from
¼ cup water

1. Combine all ingredients in food processor and process until smooth. This will take a bit of time. You will want to stop and scrape down the sides, once in a while.
2. Split mixture between three bowls.
3. To the first bowl add the ingredients for the Garlic Pepper Rosemary Spread. To the second bowl, add the ingredients for the Sun-dried Chipotle Spread. To the third bowl, add the ingredients for the Cranberry Walnut Spread.

Garlic Pepper Rosemary Spread

1 cup Base
2 cloves garlic, chopped
1 tablespoon nutritional yeast
pinch Himalayan salt
pinch pepper
1 tablespoon rosemary

1. Process with 1 cup of the base in the food processor until well mixed. Chill.

Continued...

Sun-dried Chipotle Spread

1 cup Base
½ teaspoon ground chipotle
1 teaspoon smoked paprika
¼ teaspoon Himalayan salt
1 tablespoon nutritional yeast
⅓ cup sun-dried tomatoes, softened and chopped

1.   Mix all ingredients together. Chill.

Cranberry Walnut Spread

1 cup Base
1 tablespoon agave nectar
½ cup dried cranberries
½ cup chopped walnuts

1.   Mix all ingredients together, chill.

Cranberry Walnut Crackers with Cranberry-Orange Spread

What do you get when you put together walnuts, cranberries, oranges and flax seeds? Super healthy raw food crackers that are festive and full of flavor! These beauties are packed with nutrients and are perfect for your holiday table. Pair them with the Cranberry Orange Spread and you have a healthy, raw food holiday treat that is great for entertaining or just family snacking.

Walnuts are considered one of the healthiest nuts available. They are loaded with omega 3´s, protect the cardiovascular system, and support cognitive function and the immune system. They are anti-inflammatory, and have many cancer preventing properties.

Cranberries are off the charts with health benefits. Scientific studies have shown that they are good for your heart, full of anti-oxidants, and can help prevent both urinary tract and yeast infections. They can help elevate your HDL (good) cholesterol and lower your bad cholesterol. Cranberries are also anti bacterial and help with oral and gastrointestinal health.

You can serve these crackers to your family and guests, knowing that you are not only providing them with great nutrients, but also tons of flavor!

Continued...

Cranberry Walnut Crackers with Cranberry Orange Spread continued...

Cranberry Walnut Crackers

2 cups fresh cranberries, coarsely chopped
1 cup orange juice, from fresh oranges
¼ cup agave nectar
4 cups walnuts, soaked overnight and drained
1 cup ground flax

1. Place roughly chopped cranberries in bag with orange juice and agave. Marinate for 2 hours.
2. Place walnuts in food processor. Process until finely chopped.
3. Add cranberries, agave and orange juice and pulse until cranberries are well combined.
4. Add flax and pulse until combined.
5. Spread on nonstick sheets about ¼-inch. Score.
6. Dehydrate at 145 for 45 minutes then 116 for 3 hours. Peel off sheets and continue to dry until done. (6-8 more hours).

Cranberry Orange Spread

1 cup fresh cranberries
1 cup cashews, soaked overnight, drained
½ cup flesh from young Thai coconut
1 orange, juice and zest
3 tablespoon agave nectar

1. Place cranberries in processor and coarsely chop. Remove from processor and set aside.
2. Place cashews, coconut flesh, orange juice, orange zest and agave in food processor. Process until very blended.
3. Remove and stir in chopped cranberries. Makes about 2 cups.

crackers, breads, and bars

BBQ Crackers

*P*eople often ask, "What is the one raw food item that you wouldn't want to be without?" For me, it is flatbread and crackers. I always make sure that there are some in the cupboard, and never wait for the first batch to be gone before starting a new one.

I love this raw food recipe because of its versatility. Throw on a few veggies or sprouts and you have a healthy snack. They are also great with spreads and make beautiful appetizers. This recipe for BBQ crackers is one of my favorites. They have great texture—not super hard like a lot of the crackers; they have a nice mouth feel.

MAKES 1 ½ TRAYS

1 cup flax seed
2 cups water
1 cup almonds, soaked, dehydrated, and ground fine in the food processor
1 cup raw oat flour
2 tablespoons olive oil
2 tablespoons BBQ spice mix

1. Place flax seed in the water and soak until soft. This will take at least 1 hour.
2. Combine soaked flax seeds with other ingredients, spread about ¼ inch thick on a nonstick dehydrator sheet.
3. Score into squares. Dehydrate at 145 degrees for 30 minutes and then reduce to 115 and dehydrate until dry. You will want to remove to screens halfway through the drying process.

*Chef's Note: Make sure your BBQ spice mix only contains herbs and spices. Many put additives and sugar in them.

Corn Kale Chips with Chunky Guacamole

Corn Kale Chips

4 cups fresh or frozen corn, separated
2 packed cups kale, chopped
1 clove garlic
½ lime, juice from
½ cup flax seeds, ground
pinch Himalayan salt

1. Place 2 cups of corn, garlic, and lime juice in food processor. Puree. Remove to large bowl.
2. Place remaining 2 cups of corn in food processor and process until pureed. Add kale. Pulse until chopped fine and well combined. You may have to scrape down the sides of the processor a few times.
3. Add corn kale mix to corn mix in large bowl. Stir to combine.
4. Add ground flax and salt. Mix well.
5. Spread ¼ inch thick on nonstick dehydrator sheets and score. Dehydrate at 145 degrees for 45 minutes. Turn down temperature to 115 degrees and dehydrate until dry and crisp. Approximately 12 hours in you will want to flip them halfway through the dehydration and move to a screen.

Chunky Guacamole

2–3 avocados, cubed
2 tomatoes, cubed
½ onion, chopped
1 lime, juice from
Himalayan salt and pepper, to taste

1. Toss everything together in a bowl, stir to mix, and serve!

Chocolate Craisin Pecan Bread

I created this recipe when I found myself with an abundance of sprouted wheat berries on my hands. I adore sprouted grain flatbreads, and wanted one that would provide a healthy way to satisfy those sweet-tooth cravings later in the evening. Cacao gives this nice little dessert bread that wonderful chocolate flavor, and the cranberries and pecans add sweetness and amazing health benefits!

MAKES APPROXIMATELY 2 SHEETS

3 cups sprouted wheat berries
¼ cup cacao powder
¼ cup agave nectar
1 cup craisins
¾ cup chopped pecans

1. Place wheat berries in food processor and process until mashed.
2. Add cacao powder and agave. Pulse a few times to combine.
3. Add craisins and pecans. Pulse quickly to combine, but do not overprocess the craisins and pecans.
4. Spread ¼ inch thick on nonstick dehydrator sheets and score. Dehydrate at 145 degrees for 30 minutes. Turn down temperature to 115 degrees and dehydrate until dry and crisp, approximately 12 hours. You will want to flip and move to a screen halfhway through the dehydration process.

Hazelnut Cranberry Flatbread

1 cup fresh cranberries
½ cup hazelnuts
½ cup pumpkin seeds, soaked 2 hours
1 cup sprouted wheat berries flour (see page 125)
½ cup flax seeds, ground
1 cup filtered water
2 tablespoons agave nectar (or sweetener of choice)

1. Coarsely chop cranberries in food processor. Transfer to bowl.
2. Place hazel nuts and pumpkin seeds in food processor, process until well chopped. Not all the way to fine. Place in bowl with cranberries.
3. Add wheat flour and flax. Stir to combine.
4. Add water and agave, stir to combine.
5. Spread ¼ inch thick on nonstick dehydrator sheet. Score the dough. Dehydrate 1 hour at 145 degrees, reduce heat, and dehydrate for another 4 hours at 115 degrees. Flip onto mesh screen and continue to dehydrate until dry (4–6 more hours depending on your dehydrator).

Honey Cayenne Almond Butter

1 cup almonds
1 ½ tablespoons walnut (or other cold pressed oil)
1 tablespoon water (if needed)
pinch of cayenne
1 tablespoon raw honey

1. Combine almonds and oil in food processor. Process until smooth.
2. Add water as needed. Stir in by hand, cayenne and honey, if desired.

Onion Sunflower Flatbread

When eating a raw food diet, it's always a good idea to have a selection of flatbreads handy. They are fairly quick to make (other than the dehydration time), nutritious, and can be used for many things. Throw some veggies on one for a quick lunch, spread some cashew vegan cheese on another for a quick snack, and use them with raw dips for a quick, fresh treat. They are versatile!

MAKES 2 SHEETS

3 cups sprouted wheat berries
1 sweet onion coarsely chopped
¼ cup Nama Shoyu
1 cup raw sunflower seeds

1. Place sprouted wheat berries in food processor. Process until a mash like consistency is achieved.
2. Add Nama Shoyu, and onion. Process until combined but chunks of onion are still visible.
3. Stir in by hand, the sunflower seeds.
4. Spread ¼ inch thick on nonstick dehydrator sheet. Score the dough. Dehydrate 1 hour at 145, reduce heat and dehydrate for another 4 hours at 115. Flip onto mesh screen, and continue to dehydrate until dry 4-6 more hours depending on your dehydrator.

Pumpkin Seed Crackers

3 cups sprouted wheat berries
1 cup flax seeds, ground fine
¼ cup Nama Shoyu
1 purple onion, chopped
2 cloves garlic
½ cup pumpkin seeds

1. Place sprouted wheat berries in food processor and process until meal like consistency is achieved.
2. Add ground flax seeds, Nama Shoyu and pulse until combined.
3. Add onion and garlic. Process until well combined and no chunks of onion are present.
4. Spread on nonstick sheet and top with pumpkin seeds. Press the seeds into the mixture, sprinkle with Himalayan salt and score.
5. Spread ¼ inch thick on nonstick dehydrator sheet. Score the dough. Dehydrate 1 hour at 145, reduce heat and dehydrate for another 4 hours at 115. Flip onto mesh screen, and continue to dehydrate until dry 4-6 more hours depending on your dehydrator.

Raw Goji Cacao Energy Bars

Need some quick energy to get moving in the morning? Or a fast afternoon pick me up? These bars are the perfect thing for that. Tasty, sweet, and made with super healthy ingredients, they not only satisfy your hunger, they also provide easily accessible, high-nutrient energy to get or keep you going.

Almonds are high in protein, zinc, and calcium. They are also a great source of vitamin E, magnesium, calcium, potassium, and iron. Considered a super food, pumpkin seeds are full of magnesium, which keeps bones strong, promotes healthy heart function, and supports your nervous system's function. They are also packed with protein, B vitamins, and are a good source of iron, zinc, and fiber!

Golden flax seeds contain 27 cancer preventing substances, as well as omega-3's, which are great in the battle against heart disease. Goji berries are high in protein, amino acids and are packed with antioxidants. Cacao nibs are partially ground cacao beans. They are full of antioxidants and trace minerals and will give you a little pick me up, too!

1 cup almonds, soaked overnight and drained
1 cup pumpkin seeds, soaked
1 cup flax seeds, soaked in 1 ½ cup water
⅓ cup agave nectar
1 teaspoon cinnamon
½ cup goji berries
½ cup cacao nibs

1. Soak almonds, pumpkin seeds, and flax seeds for at least 6 hours. Drain almonds and pumpkin seeds.
2. Place almonds and pumpkin seeds in food processor. Process until well ground but still chunky.

3. Add agave and cinnamon, pulse until well combined.
4. Remove from food processor and place in large bowl. Add flax seeds, cacao nibs, and goji berries, stir.
5. Press into a rectangle on nonstick dehydrator sheet. You want these to be ½ inch thick.
6. Dehydrate at 145 degrees for 45 minutes. Reduce heat and dehydrate for 3 more hours.
7. Peel off dehydrator sheet, dehydrate for 2 more hours. At this point, you will remove them from the dehydrator, cut into bars, separate so there is a little space in between each bar, and return to dehydrator for 2–3 more hours. You want them dry but not brittle. They should be a little soft.
8. Top with raw chocolate (see page 91).

Raw Chocolate

1 cup raw cacao butter
1 teaspoon vanilla
3 tablespoons coconut oil, melted
⅓ cup powdered Sucanat, finely ground in coffee grinder
2 tablespoons agave nectar
7 ounces cacao powder

1. Melt cacao butter and coconut oil in dehydrator or over hot water.
2. In food processor, combine melted cacao butter, coconut oil, and vanilla. Remove half of the mixture and set aside.
3. Add half of the cacao powder and combine.
4. Add Sucanat and combine.
5. Add agave and remaining coconut butter/oil mixture that was set aside and combine.
6. Add remaining cacao powder, mix well. It should be quite liquid at this point. It will harden as it cools.

Spicy Flax Crackers

MAKES 2 SHEETS

3 cups flax seeds, soaked in 5 ½ cups water for at least 3 hours
1 tablespoon dried mustard
¼ cup agave nectar
1 shallot, chopped
1 clove garlic, chopped
3 tablespoons Numa Shoyu

1. Place all ingredients in food processor. Process until well combined.
2. Spread ¼ inch thick on nonstick dehydrator sheet. Score the dough. Dehydrate 1 hour at 145 degees, reduce heat, and dehydrate for another 4 hours at 115 degees. Flip onto mesh screen and continue to dehydrate until dry (4–6 more hours depending on your dehydrator).

Sesame Flax Crackers

MAKES 2 SHEETS

1 cup flax seeds
2 cups water
1 cup raw oat flour
½ cup water
2 teaspoons dehydrated onion flakes
1 teaspoon Himalayan salt
¼ cup black sesame seeds

1. Soak flax seeds in water for 3+ hours, drain.
2. Mix soaked flax seeds together with oat flour, water, onion flakes, and salt.
3. Spread on nonstick dehydrator sheets about ¼ inch thick. Sprinkle sesame seeds on top and score with knife. Dehydrate at 145 degrees for 30 minutes then reduce to 115 degrees for 2 hours. Remove nonstick sheets and place top up on screens. Dehydrate at least 2–4 more hours or until dry.

Strawberry Banana Treats

There are two raw food recipe questions that come up frequently. One is, "What do you do with the leftover pulp when you make nut milks?" and the second, "Do you have any raw food recipes for kid's snacks?" I thought I would tackle both of them with the same recipe! Using the dehydrated pulp from my almond milk and a combination of strawberries and bananas (always a favorite of my girls), I threw together these quick little snack "cookies." They are tasty, super healthy, and your kids will love them. No artificial colors, flavors, or white stuff!

MAKES 1 ½ TRAYS

1 banana
1 cup strawberries
1 cup almond flour
1 cup raw flaked oats
1 tablespoon agave nectar (optional)
1 tablespoon coconut oil, softened
5 large strawberries, sliced thin

1. Place banana, strawberries, agave, and coconut oil in food processor and blend until smooth.
2. Add almond flour and pulse until combined.
3. Hand stir in flaked oats.
4. Spread on nonstick a little less than ¼ inch thick. Score and top each square with strawberry slice. Dehydrate at 145 degrees for 30 minutes and then 115 degrees for 2 hours. Move to mesh screens and dehydrate until dry but not hard. You want these to be a little soft. Refrigerate.

Tomato Flatbread

2 cups soaked wheat berries (oat groats can be substituted)
1 cup almonds, soaked overnight, and drained
1 cup flax seeds, ground
1 clove garlic
1 cup tomato puree (from fresh tomatoes)
1 cup water

1. The night before, soak almonds and grain (separately).
2. Start food processor and drop in garlic.
3. Once it is processed, add almonds. Process until well ground. Remove to large bowl.
4. Put wheat or oat groats in processor. Process until a mash is made.
5. Put in bowl with almonds and garlic.
6. Add flax and combine.
7. Add water and tomato puree.
8. Mix well. Spread on nonstick sheets to about ¼ inch thick. Score. Dehydrate for 1 hour at 145 degrees. Reduce heat to 115 degrees and continue to dry for 2 more hours. Peel sheets off and continue to dry (tops up) until dry. This can take 6 hours or more depending on your dehydrator, humidity, etc.

Spicy Corn Chips

6 cups frozen corn, thawed
1 red pepper
2 limes, juice from
2 teaspoons cayenne pepper
1 teaspoon smoked paprika
pinch Himalayan salt

1. Blend all ingredients in food processor.
2. Spread on nonstick sheet at least ¼ inch thick as these will really dehydrate down.
3. Score into the shape you desire.
4. Dehydrate at 145 degrees for 1 hour, reduce heat to 115 degrees and dehydrate for 10 hours. Pull off of the nonstick sheet and dry until very dry. Place right side up as chips will curl if you flip them.

Zucchini Carrot Bread

The flatbreads that I make in the dehydrator have become a staple of my raw food diet. They are easy to make, and can store for weeks. Nutritionally, they dramatically outshine any type of "baked" bread or cracker. They are so convenient they could be considered "fast" raw food. There is a little preparation that goes into making the breads, but once you get into the rhythm of making them, you will be surprised at how easy it is to incorporate flatbreads into your diet.

Flatbreads can be savory or sweet. Look at the ingredients and you will be amazed at both how simple and healthy they are. This bread started out with sprouted wheat berries as its base. Sprouting grains brings out the highest nutritional value that they possess. Grains will take 2–4 days to sprout, so plan accordingly. I normally have some type of sprouted seeds or grains "cooking" all the time.

MAKES APPROXIMATELY 1 ½ SHEETS

3 cups sprouted wheat berries
1 cup flax seeds, ground
3 small zucchini, chopped
3 carrots, chopped
1 shallot, chopped

1. Place carrots in food processor and process to small dice and set aside.
2. Place wheat berries in food processor. Process until berries start to form a mash.
3. Add flax seeds and zucchini (cut into chunks). Process until zucchini becomes incorporated.
4. Add carrots and shallot (cut into small chunks). Process the whole mixture until everything is incorporated and in a very small dice.
5. Mix well. Spread on nonstick sheets to about ¼ inch thick. Score. Dehydrate for 1 hour at 145 degrees. Reduce heat to 115 degrees and continue to dry for 2 more hours. Peel sheets off and continue to dry (tops up) until dry. This can take 6 hours or more depending on your dehydrator, humidity, etc.

Cinnamon Pomegranate Flatbread

I love to have something a little sweet for breakfast. I think it comes from my days of sugar-coated cereal and oatmeal with brown sugar and butter. There's hardly any grain left in these meals! Today, I take that grain, sprout it, and make it into beautiful fruit-infused breads.

Cinnamon pomegranate bread topped with strawberry cashew cream and a bit of fruit provides a quick, easy, and satisfying breakfast. This is a bread that should be dried with just a little moisture left in. Don't worry about using the whole seeds from the pomegranate, they incorporate beautifully.

MAKES 2 SHEETS

3 cups sprouted wheat berries
1 cup flax seeds, ground
1 teaspoon cinnamon
2 pomegranates, seeds from
¼ cup agave nectar

1. Place wheat berries in the food processor. Process until berries start to form a mash.
2. Add cinnamon, ground flax, and pomegranate seeds. Process until seeds are incorporated and somewhat ground up. If you would like a little extra sweetness, add agave.
3. Dehydrate on nonstick sheets for 8 hours, flip and dehydrate until bread is mostly dry but not completely hard. Store in refrigerator.

Onion Flax Crackers

MAKES 2 SHEETS

2 cups flax seeds, soaked in 3 ½ cups water at least 3 hours
1 cup flax seeds, ground
1 sweet onion, coarsely chopped
1 clove garlic, chopped
¼ cup Nama Shoyu
½ cup hemp seeds

1. Place all ingredients in food processor. Process until well combined.
2. Spread ¼ inch thick on nonstick dehydrator sheet. Score the dough. Dehydrate 1 hour at 145 degrees, reduce heat, and dehydrate for another 4 hours at 115 degees. Flip onto mesh screen and continue to dehydrate until dry (4–6 more hours, depending on your dehydrator).

salads

Avocado Mango Broccoli Salad

*Y*ears ago, there was a dessert that I would occasionally treat myself to. It involved a brownie, a scoop of ice cream, a cast-iron skillet, hot fudge, and hot caramel sauce. The brownie and the caramel sauce were heated in the oven until sizzling. They were topped with the ice cream and hot fudge. What made this dessert so special was the combination of hot and cold and the opposing textures of smooth and crunchy. Opposing textures apply to all food. They create a more interesting mouth feel and are a simple way to add complexity. This quick and easy salad uses opposing textures and flavors, and the result is divine.

In the summer heat, salad for dinner is an appetizing alternative to heavier meals. A dinner salad requires some substance. Avocados and mangoes are a great flavor combination but very similar in texture. By adding broccoli and a red onion, you introduce the crunch and a big nutritional boost. Broccoli provides vitamin A, C, folic acid, and a healthy dose of calcium, magnesium, and iron. Broccoli also contains indoles, which can neutralize harmful estrogens that promote tumor growth; sulforaphane, which stimulates cells to make cancer-fighting enzymes, and beta-carotene, which is another known cancer fighter. Broccoli contains 26 percet protein and a healthy dose of calcium.

2 ripe avocados
2 ripe mangoes
2–3 cups broccoli, chopped
½ cup red onion, chopped
¾ cup raisins
Himalayan salt and pepper, to taste

1.   Combine all ingredients. Chill and serve!

Broccoli Raisin Sunflower Seed Salad

MAKES 4–6 SERVINGS

Dressing

1 cup cashews, soaked 6 hours and drained
1 ½ lemons, juice from
2 tablespoons olive oil
¼ cup water
1 shallot, chopped
1 clove garlic
2 tablespoons agave nectar
½ tablespoon mustard powder
pinch Himalayan salt

1. Combine all ingredients in high-speed blender. Mix until silky smooth.

Salad

6 cups broccoli, chopped
½ medium red onion, chopped
1 cup raisins
1 cup raw sunflower seeds
dressing

1. Mix together broccoli, onion, raisins, and sunflower seeds.
2. Top with dressing and combine until well coated.

Jicama Salad

*I*f you haven't had jicama, you are missing out on a real treat. Jicama has a texture somewhere between a potato and a pear, with a slight sweetness. It is 86–90 percent water and is very hydrating. It has a very mild taste, somewhat reminiscent of apples, and makes a great addition to salads. High in vitamin C and with no fat, 1 cup contains only 45 calories. Enjoy it in this salad with a flavorful curry peanut sauce. This is a summer favorite around our house.

1 large jicama, cubed
1 cup pea pods, chopped
2 scallions, sliced
½ cup raisins
½ Peanut Curry Sauce

1. Peel and cut jicama into ½-inch pieces.
2. Cut pea pods into ½-inch pieces.
3. Combine jicama, pea pods, raisins, and scallions. Stir in Peanut Curry Sauce

Peanut Curry Sauce

¾ cup peanuts, soaked 2 hours, drained
1 young Thai coconut, flesh from
¼ cup coconut water, from young coconut
2 teaspoons curry powder
pinch Himalayan salt

1. Open young coconut and drain water out. Reserve water.
2. Remove flesh. Place ¼ cup coconut water in blender or high-speed blender. Add the flesh from the coconut, raw peanuts, curry powder, and salt.
3. Combine until smooth.

Brussels Sprouts with Figs

*I*t all started with a conversation on Facebook. One of my friends asked if anyone had a recipe for brussels sprouts. I love brussels sprouts. I think my love for them started when I used them as Barbie cabbages. I used to beg my mom to give me some so Barbie could cook too. So, the next time I went to the farmer's market, one of my goals was to score some brussels sprouts!

The brussels sprouts I found were little bitty ones. Quite cute, but very small. They would have made great Barbie cabbages. Raw brussels sprouts can be very bitter, so I knew that if I was going to make a raw food recipe with them, I would have to enlist the dehydrator. I made a marinade of olive oil, garlic, a little lemon juice, and salt and pepper. I let them sit for a bit, and then popped them in the dehydrator. After about 6 hours they were done.

I also had a box of figs that I had picked up earlier in the day. After tasting the brussels sprouts, I decided they were just OK. Something was missing. I looked at the figs and then back at the brussels sprouts. Were the figs the missing piece? I tried it and it was magic. The sweetness of the figs complemented the brussels sprouts beautifully.

MAKES 4 SERVINGS

3 cups brussels sprouts, *halved (quartered if they are very large)*
1 cup fresh figs, quartered
⅓ cup olive oil
1 clove garlic, pressed
1 teaspoon lemon juice
Himalayan salt, to taste
pepper, to taste

1. Whisk together all ingredients except brussels sprouts to make marinade.
2. Add brussels sprouts to marinade. Toss to coat well.
3. Place in dehydrator at 115 degrees for 6 hours.
4. Remove from dehydrator and mix in quartered figs.

Chia Fruit Salad

1 apple, chopped
1 orange, chopped
¼ cup blueberries
½ cup unsweetened craisins
½ cup walnuts
½ cup flaked coconut (unsweetened)

Dressing

1 lemon, juice from
3 tablespoons agave nectar
1 tablespoon chia seeds

1. Combine all salad ingredients.
2. Whisk the lemon juice into the agave, stir in the chia seeds, and pour over salad. Mix to combine.

Fall Slaw with Maple Tahini Dressing

Slaw

MAKES 4 SERVINGS

2 apples, 1 chopped, 1 grated
½ lemon
2 carrots
1 rutabaga, peeled and shredded
1 kohlrabi, peeled and shredded
2 stalks celery, sliced
1 cup dried cranberries
¾ cup pumpkin seeds

1. Place apples in bowl. Squeeze the juice from ½ lemon over the apples and stir.
2. Add the rest of ingredients and stir to combine.

Maple Tahini Dressing

¾ cup tahini
½ cup water
1 lemon, juice from
2 teaspoons fresh ginger, grated
3 tablespoons maple syrup, yakon syrup, or agave nectar
   pinch Himalayan salt (optional)

1. Whisk all ingredients together.
2. Pour over slaw and mix well.

Sunflower Pumpkin Turmeric Salad

MAKES 4 SERVINGS

¾ cup pumpkin seeds, soaked overnight, rinsed, and drained
¾ cup sunflower seeds, soaked overnight, rinsed, and drained
½ cup sweet onion, chopped
1 cup celery, chopped
2 cups jicama, chopped
1 cup cucumber, chopped
1 cup raisins

1. Place pumpkin seeds and sunflower seeds in food processor. Pulse about 5–10 times to coarsely chop the seeds.
2. Remove from food processor and place in bowl.
3. Add all other ingredients. Stir.
4. Stir in dressing.

Dressing

½ cup Brazil nuts, soaked 3 hours and
   drained
2 dates
2 teaspoons turmeric
¼ cup water

1. Place Brazil nuts, dates, turmeric, and water in high-speed blender. Blend until smooth.

Marinated Kale Salad

Marinade

MAKES 4 SERVINGS

1 clove garlic, finely diced
1 lemon, juice from (about 3 tablespoons)
1 tablespoon agave nectar (you can substitute your favorite sweetener)
pinch Himalayan salt
pinch pepper
¼ cup flax seed oil

1. Whisk together the garlic, lemon juice, agave, salt, and pepper.
2. Slowly pour oil into the mixture while still whisking. Set aside.

Salad

1 bunch kale (I used dinosaur kale for this recipe)
1 cup cherry tomatoes
2 avocados, chopped
¼ head purple cabbage, chopped
¼ purple onion, diced
¼ cup hemp seeds

1. Remove stems from kale leaves and tear into bite-sized pieces.
2. Combine kale with marinade. Massage for a few minutes to well coat, set aside.
3. Prepare tomatoes, avocados, cabbage, and onion.
4. Stir into kale mixture and mix well.
5. Top with hemp seeds and mix in.

Spinach with Tarragon Pine Nut Sauce

*H*ow wonderful it is when life throws something completely unexpected your way. Recently, I was shopping at a local cooking store. Having sent the sales person off to look for some small tart pans, I went back to being completely distracted by all the cooking gadgets surrounding me. "How are things?" Looking up I instantly realized that the woman checking on my tart pans was a former bridesmaid of mine! She was a dear friend that I had lost contact with over the years. She didn't recognize me either, and we both had a good laugh. Connections made, we were thrilled!

After much catching up, we started talking about raw food. Kim is a very good cook and was quite interested to learn about the health benefits and techniques used to make raw food. What followed was an entire day of raw food creating. She brought some of her favorite recipes and we converted them with fabulous results. For lunch, raw wilted spinach salad with pine nut tarragon hit the spots and she was pleased to see how easy it was to prepare. For one of her first raw meals, it went well.

Pine Nut Sauce

2 cups pine nuts, soaked 1 hour
½ lemon, juice from
1 small clove garlic
1 small shallot
2 tablespoons olive oil
3 tablespoons fresh tarragon, chopped
pinch Himalayan salt
fresh ground pepper, to taste

1. Place all ingredients except tarragon in food processor and blend very well.
2. Add chopped tarragon and pulse a few times to mix.

Salad

5 cups raw spinach
1 cup cherry tomatoes, halved

1. To make a "wilted" spinach, rub handfuls of spinach with your fingers until desired texture is achieved.
2. Mix in Pine Nut Tarragon Sauce (you won't need all of the sauce, add by spoonful until you achieve your desired amount) and tomatoes, stir.

Strawberry Mango Salad

MAKES 2–4 SERVINGS

1 head romaine lettuce
1 cup strawberries, sliced
1 cup mango, diced
1 cup jicama, diced
1 avocado, diced
1 cup pumpkin seeds

1. Tear romaine and place on plate.
2. Mix together fruit and jicama. Place a handful on the lettuce bed.
3. Top with Blueberry Vinaigrette and pumpkin seeds.

Blueberry Vinaigrette

1 cup blueberries
1 tablespoon agave nectar (or sweetener of your choice)
2 tablespoons red wine vinegar
¼ cup olive oil, cold pressed

1. Combine all ingredients in a blender.
2. Pour over top of salad.

Orange Pomegranate Salad

When the holidays are over and the tables full of beautiful, festive food are gone, I often find myself conflicted. While my body is craving clean, healthy raw food, my mind still is looking for beauty. Time for a festive salad! Oranges, pomegranate, pecans, and greens topped with an orange chia-seed dressing. Quick, festive, and delicious!

MAKES 2-4 SERVINGS

2 cups romaine lettuce
1 orange
1 cup pomegranate seeds
½ cup pecans, chopped

1. Tear romaine and place on plate in a circle.
2. Remove the membranes from the orange slices and place on top of the romaine.
3. Sprinkle with the pomegranate seeds and top with the pecan pieces.
4. Pour dressing over top.

Orange Chia-Seed Dressing

1 orange, juice from
1 tablespoon agave nectar
1 tablespoon chia seeds

1. Whisk all ingredients and pour on top of salad.

Strawberry Summer Salad

Summer is the time to celebrate locally grown produce. Strawberries take on a whole new personality when they are grown close by. The berries' deep red flesh bursts in your mouth with flavor. Evoking picnics by the lake, bare feet, and sweet fragrant breezes, local strawberries are truly a summer indulgence.

In late summer, salads can become the focal point of the meal. Heavier foods are no longer appealing as the long, warm days ask us for a refreshing meal. Strawberries are a wonderful addition to greens. Combined with a raw strawberry vinaigrette and almond brittle for an extra textural crunch, this salad will easily take center stage.

This recipe requires advanced prep time for the almond brittle.

Salad

4 cups greens of choice
Strawberry Vinaigrette
16 strawberries, halved

Strawberry Vinaigrette

8 medium strawberries
1 cup olive oil
¼ cup agave nectar
2 lemons, juice from

1. Place all ingredients in high-speed blender and blend until smooth and emulsified. Makes ½ cup.

Almond Brittle

1 cup almonds, soaked overnight, rinsed, and drained
2 teaspoons cinnamon
½ teaspoon ginger
pinch cayenne pepper
2 –3 tablespoons maple syrup

1. Drain almonds and pat dry.
2. Place all ingredients in food processor. Process until well ground but some larger chunks still exist. If you need more moisture to hold together, add the extra maple syrup.
3. Flatten out on a nonstick sheet. Dehydrate for 8 hours or until brittle is very dry.
4. Carefully break into pieces.

Assembly

1. Place salad in center of plate. Surround with sliced strawberries.
2. Drizzle vinaigrette on salad, top with crumbled almond brittle.

main
dishes

Zucchini Basil Wraps

I love wraps. They are a quick, easy way to throw together a tasty, healthy lunch or dinner. These wraps have a zucchini-basil base with a little coconut thrown in. Black sesame seeds add some color and nutrients. For the filling, a quick dice of some veggies combined with spinach cream is perfect. These are quick, easy and bursting with flavor. The wraps will keep in the refrigerator for a few weeks, if properly wrapped.

MAKES ENOUGH FILLING FOR 4–6 WRAPS

3 cups zucchini, chopped
1 young Thai coconut, flesh from
¾ cup ground flax seeds, ground
12 leaves fresh basil
pinch Himalayan salt
pinch ground pepper
black sesame seeds

1. Place all ingredients except black sesame seeds in blender. Blend until smooth.
2. Spread in a thin layer on nonstick sheets. Don't spread too thin or you will have holes.
3. Sprinkle sesame seeds on top.
4. Dehydrate at 115 degrees for 3 hours.
5. When tops are dry, peel off of sheet and dry until bottoms are dry to the touch but still pliable. Cut into 5-inch squares.

Continued…

Spinach Cream Dressing

1 cup macadamia nuts
½ cup water
1 cup young Thai coconut flesh
1 clove garlic
2 cups raw spinach
½ lemon, juice from
pinch Himalayan salt
pinch pepper

1. Place all ingredients in high-speed blender and blend until smooth.

Assembly

2 carrots, cubed
2 cucumbers, cubed
2 avocados, cubed
2 tomatoes, cubed
1 cup jicama, cubed

1. Mix all vegetables together.
2. Add Spinach Cream Dressing to the mixture by spoonful to taste. Combine.
3. Place a layer of lettuce on the wrap. Spoon filling on lettuce and wrap up.

Broccoli Mushroom "Stir Fry"

Marinade

SERVES 2–4

¼ cup olive oil
2 tablespoons Nama Shoyu
1 tablespoon agave nectar or raw honey

1. Whisk olive oil, Nama Shoyu, and agave or honey together.

Stir Fry

SERVES 2–4

1 ½ cups sliced mushrooms
1 cup broccoli, chopped
1 large parsnip
2 carrots
1 cup pea pods
sesame oil (optional)
black sesame seeds (optional)

1. Place mushrooms and broccoli in marinade. Stir to coat. Set aside.
2. Peel and cut parsnip into pieces. Place in food processor and process until coarsely chopped.
3. Cut the carrots into matchstick-sized pieces.
4. Chop the pea pods into ½-inch pieces and mix into the parsnip "rice" with the carrots.
5. Stir in the entire broccoli- mushroom marinade mix. Toss. You can dress it with a little sesame oil and black sesame seeds for more flavor.

Basil Veggie Primavera

*T*his recipe starts with a simple basil oil and a basil-cashew-walnut spread. These simple building blocks can convert into a couple of different meals. A simple spread for veggies or flatbread and also a wonderful sauce for a raw "pasta" primavera.

The primavera is a very quick and delicious way to use the basil-walnut-cashew spread and turn it into a refreshing, satisfying dinner! A little additional basil oil and some filtered water thins the spread into a sauce. Chop up some veggies and you are good to go. Dinner in under 5 minutes!

Basil Oil

2 cups packed basil
1 cup cold-pressed olive oil

1.   Place basil and oil in blender.
2.   Blend until well combined.
3.   Strain.

Basil-Walnut-Cashew Spread

2 cups cashews, soaked overnight, rinsed, and drained
½ cup walnuts, soaked overnight, rinsed, and drained
½ cup filtered water
2 tablespoons Basil Oil (see above)
2 cloves garlic
1 teaspoon lemon juice
pinch Himalayan salt
pinch ground pepper

1.   Place all ingredients in food processor. Process until well blended.

Continued…

Basil Veggie Primavera continued...

Sauce

½ cup Basil-Walnut-Cashew Spread
¼ cup filtered water
2 tablespoons Basil Oil

1. Whisk water and Basil Oil into Basil-Walnut-Cashew Spread.

Primavera

SERVES 2–3 (CAN EASILY BE DOUBLED)

1 cup carrots
1 cup zucchini
1 cup yellow squash
1 cup cherry tomatoes, halved
Basil-Walnut-Cashew Spread

1. Chop carrots, zucchini, and yellow squash into bite-sized pieces.
2. Stir in tomatoes.
3. Top with sauce and mix to coat.
4. Optional: top with chiffonade basil (thinly sliced), Himalayan salt, and pepper to taste.

*Chef's Note: This sauce has a brownish tinge to it from the walnuts. If you want a white sauce, replace the walnuts with more cashews. But they are so darn healthy, I would use them!

Chipotle Corn Soup

4–5 cups fresh corn (approximately 6 ears)
1 ½ cups filtered water
¼ teaspoon chipotle
pinch Himalayan salt
pinch smoked paprika (optional)

1. Place all ingredients in high-speed blender. Blend until well combined.
2. Strain through strainer. (You may have to assist the liquid through the strainer by stirring it.)
3. Serve topped with a pinch of the smoked paprika (optional) and Kale Chips (see page 41).

Raw "BLTs"

Raw Honey Wheat Bread

SERVES 2

2 cups wheat berries, sprouted and ground into flour
1 cup zucchini puree
1 apple
1 tablespoon honey
1 cup ground flax seeds, ground

1. To make flour: Soak wheat berries for 24 hours, then rinse 2 times a day until small tails sprout. Dehydrate at 116 degrees until dry. Grind into flour.
2. In food processor, place apple, zucchini puree, and honey. Process until a puree is achieved.
3. Mix together flour and ground flax.
4. Stir puree mixture into flour mixture.
5. Spread ¼ inch thick on nonstick dehydrator sheets. Score mixture into bread-sized squares. Dehydrate at 145 degrees for 45 minutes, turn down heat and dehydrate at 115 degrees until tops are dry.
6. Flip over, remove nonstick, sheet and continue to dry. You want to make sure the bread dries but stays soft, so check and don't over dehydrate.

Continued...

Raw "BLTs" continued...

Avocado Butter

2 avocados
½ cup cashews, soaked until soft
pinch Himalayan salt
pinch black pepper
pinch ground chipotle

1. Place all ingredients in food processor and pulse until well blended.

Eggplant Bacon

(see page 46)

Assembly

Raw Honey Wheat Bread
Avocado Butter
tomato
lettuce
Eggplant Bacon

1. Layer ingredients on bread to create sandwich.

Carrot Hazelnut Soup

SERVES 2

½ cup hazelnuts
1 ½ cups water
3 cups carrots, cut into chunks
1 apple, peeled, cored, and sliced
1 tablespoon raw honey
1 teaspoon ginger
1 teaspoon cinnamon
Himalayan salt and pepper, to taste

1. Place hazelnuts and water in food processor. Process until smooth.
2. Add carrots, apple, honey, ginger, and cinnamon. Blend until smooth.
3. Salt and pepper to taste.

Falafel with Mango Pineapple Salsa

I love food. I love flavor. I love falafels! There is a great little restaurant in Boulder, CO, where you can order your falafels and choose from all kinds of sides to put with them. It is quick, yummy, and there is a wonderful outside patio where you can sit, eat, and watch the traffic on Pearl Street go by. Desperate for a raw food recipe that re-creates these tasty little favorites, I sprouted chickpeas and got to work. Paired with a raw recipe for "sour cream" and a mango salsa, this raw food recipe completely hits the spot!

Chickpeas or garbanzo beans are a great way to add a complete protein to your raw food diet. They are low glycemic, full of fiber and trace minerals, and are a good source of iron.

Falafel

SERVES 4

3 cups sprouted garbanzo beans (chick peas)
1 cup onion, chopped
2 cloves garlic
1 cup sunflower seeds
½ cup flax seeds, ground
¼ cup lemon juice
¼ cup parsley
2 tablespoons olive oil
2 teaspoons coriander
3 teaspoons cumin
1 tablespoon Nama Shoyu

1. Sprout garbanzo beans: Place 2 cups dry beans in a jar, cover with water, and let soak for 24 hours. Make sure there is plenty of room in the jar as these will expand quite a bit. Drain off water and rinse 3 times a day until little sprouts appear. Usually 2–3 days.

Continued....

Falafel with Mango Pineapple Salsa continued...

2. Place sunflower seeds in food processor and grind until fine. Place ground sunflower seeds in large bowl.
3. With food processor running, drop 2 cloves of garlic in. Let run until garlic has been chopped.
4. Place sprouted garbanzo beans in food processor with garlic. Process until a mash is achieved. Remove to bowl with sunflower seeds.
5. Chop onion in food processor, pulsing until a very fine chop is achieved. Place in bowl with garbanzo bean mixture.
6. Chop parsley and add along with remaining ingredients to bean mixture. Combine well.
7. Shape into golf-sized balls and dehydrate, beginning at 145 degrees for 1 hour and then reducing heat to 115 degrees for 4–6 hours. You will want to check as they dehydrate. They should be crispy on the outside but still a little soft on the inside.

Mango Pineapple Salsa

1 cup pineapple, diced
1 cup mango, diced
1 jicama, diced
½ cup onion, diced
3 teaspoons cilantro, finely chopped
1 lime, juice from

1. Mix all ingredients together. Let sit to marinate.

Continued...

Sour Cream

¼ cup cashews, soaked overnight and drained
1 young Thai coconut, flesh from (about ¾ cup)
2 tablespoons lemon juice
pinch Himalayan salt

1. Combine all ingredients in blender until smooth. You can add water to thin if needed.

Assembly

1 cup alfalfa sprouts
Falafel
Pineapple Mango Salsa
Sour Cream

Create a bed of alfalfa sprouts, place Falafel on top of the sprouts. Top with Sour Cream and serve with Salsa.

Mushroom Walnut Veggie Burgers

I have been wanting to make a raw food burger for quite a while now. Finding a great deal on portabello mushrooms was just the dose of inspiration that I needed to put this recipe together. Filled with veggies, seeds, nuts, and hearty savory seasoning, these mushroom burgers really hit the spot. A little soaking, a little dehydrating, and you have a tasty burger that even the fussiest eater will love. If you use the food processor, these go together very quickly!

MAKES 8–9

2 cups carrots, grated
2 cups portobello mushrooms, chopped fine
1 cup onion, chopped fine
¾ cup celery, diced
1 cup walnuts, soaked, drained, and ground fine while wet
½ cup pumpkin seeds, soaked, drained, and ground fine while wet
¼ cup water, filtered
¼ cup Nama Shoyu
1 teaspoon sage
1 teaspoon marjoram
1 teaspoon thyme
1 cup raw oat flour, or ¾ cup flax seeds, ground

1. Combine carrots, mushrooms, celery, and onion.
2. Stir in walnuts and pumpkin seeds, combine well.
3. Combine water and Nama Shoyu, mix into veggie/nut mixture
4. Add herbs, stir well.
5. Stir raw oat flour or ground flax seeds in batches (half at a time).
6. Shape into patties, 4–5 inches across, no more than 1 inch thick. Place on screens and dehydrate at 145 degrees for 1 hour. Reduce heat to 115 degrees and dehydrate until mostly dry, 3–4 hours. You want these to be moist, not rock hard.

Spaghetti and "Sausage"

Mushroom Sausage

2 cups carrots, grated
2 cups portobello mushrooms, chopped fine
1 cup onion, chopped fine
¾ cup celery, diced
1 cup walnuts, soaked, drained, and ground fine while wet
½ cup pumpkin seeds, soaked, drained, and ground fine while wet
¼ cup filtered water
¼ cup Nama Shoyu
1 tablespoon Italian spices.
1 cup raw oat flour, or ¾ cup flax seeds, ground

1.   Combine carrots, mushrooms, celery, and onion.
2.   Stir in walnuts and pumpkin seeds, combine well.
3.   Combine water and Nama Shoyu, mix into veggie/nut mixture.
4.   Add herbs, stir well.
5.   Stir in raw oat flour or ground flax seeds in batches (half at a time).
6.   Shape into patties 4–5 inches across, no more than 1 inch thick. Place on screens and dehydrate at 145 degrees for 1 hour. Reduce heat and dehydrate at 115 degrees until dry, 6–8 hours. You want these to be dry.
7.   Break into bite-size pieces.

Marinara Sauce

2 cups sun-dried tomatoes
2 cups water
1 large clove garlic
1 teaspoon dried oregano
1 teaspoon dried basil
Himalayan salt and pepper, to taste

1. Soak tomatoes in water until soft.
2. Put tomatoes, water, and the rest of the ingredients in a high-speed blender.
3. Process until smooth.

Assembly:

2 yellow zucchini
Mushroom Sausage
Marinara Sauce

1. Put zucchini through spiralizer. Set in colander for 20 minutes to let water drain off.
2. Top with sauce and "sausage."

*Chef's Note: I topped this with grated pine nuts for a little extra flavor. I also like to warm this in the dehydrator prior to serving.

"Roasted" Tomato Basil Soup

MAKES 4 CUPS

4 large tomatoes, chopped
¼ mild onion, chopped
¼ cup olive oil
1 tablespoon dried oregano
1 tablespoon dried basil
pinch Himalayan salt and pepper
2 cups water
½ cup Brazil Nut Milk (see below)

1. In a large bowl, combine chopped tomatoes, onion, oil, basil, oregano, salt, and pepper. Let sit for 30 minutes. Drain.
2. Place tomatoes on nonstick sheets and dehydrate for 30 minutes at 145 degrees and then 5 ½ hours at 115 degrees.
3. Place tomatoes, onions, and water in a high-speed blender. Puree.
4. Add Brazil nut milk, quickly blend. You can lightly heat the soup in your dehydrator.

Brazil Nut Milk

1 cup Brazil nuts
4 cups water

1. Soak the nuts in the water for 6 hours. Drain and rinse.
2. Place in high-speed blender. Process until very well blended.
3. Strain through cheese cloth or nut-milk bag.

Spicy Veggie "Stir Fry"

*T*he most important raw recipes in my collection are quick and easy main dishes that really satisfy. Wanting something a little spicy and a lot flavorful, I threw some ingredients in the food processor. Tasting as I went along, I came up with one of my favorites to date. Starting with the parsnip rice, I threw in a couple more veggies and topped it off with a spicy sauce. It is fun, fast, and the flavors are great. Don't be intimidated by the parsnip rice. The flavor is very mild, and, when combined with the other ingredients, it makes a great meal.

Parsnips are full of vitamin C, have tons of fiber, and are high in folic acid. They are a good source of niacin, magnesium, thiamine, and potassium. They also have vitamins B6 and E.

Rice

2 cups parsnips, *chopped*
2 carrots
½ cup pine nuts
¾ cup broccoli, *chopped*
½ cup mushrooms, *sliced*

1. Finely chop parsnips, carrots, and pine nuts and place in bowl. If you are using a food processor to do this, you will want to do each separately.
2. Combine with chopped broccoli and sliced mushrooms.

Continued…

Spicy Veggie Stir Fry continued...

Sauce

¼ cup olive oil
⅓ cup sun-dried tomatoes, softened
1 teaspoon chili pepper powder
1 ½ teaspoon curry powder
1 tablespoon Nama Shoyu
1 tablespoon agave nectar (optional)

1. Combine all ingredients in food processor, process until well combined.
2. Stir into "rice" mixture.

Fresh Veggies with Black Beans
(Transitional Category)

3 cups cooked black beans (hot from cooking or heat if using pre-cooked)
2 cups bok choy, chopped
2 cups tomatoes, chopped
½ cups onion, chopped
1 cup fresh corn
½ lemon, juice from
2 tablespoons cilantro
½ teaspoon Himalayan salt
pepper, to taste

1. Cook black beans. I use a pressure cooker. You can also use canned beans but cooking your own is so much better! (This is a transitional recipe that uses cooked beans so it is not 100 percent raw.)
2. While beans are cooking, chop bok choy and set aside.
3. Chop onions, and tomatoes. Place in bowl.
4. Add corn to tomatoes and onions. Add lemon juice, cilantro, salt, and pepper. Stir.
5. When beans are done cooking and still hot, stir in bok choy. Let sit for a couple of minutes and then stir in the tomato mixture.

Spinach Veggie Quiche

Pumpkin Seed Pine Nut Crust

SERVES 4

1 carrot, chopped
½ shallot
1 cup pine nuts
½ cup pumpkin seeds

1. Chop carrot into 1-inch pieces and place in food processor. Process until chopped fine.
2. Add shallot and pine nuts. Pulse a few times to start to blend.
3. Add pumpkin seeds. Process until you have a formable mass but not so much that you lose the integrity of all the seeds. I like to see chunks of them.
4. Dehydrate at 145 degrees for 30 minutes. Reduce heat and dehydrate 6 hours at 115 degrees.

Continued...

Spinach Cashew Cheese Spread

1 cup cashews, soaked overnight and drained
1 ½ lemons, juice from
¼ cup olive oil
1 shallot, chopped
1 clove garlic, chopped
½ cup sun-dried tomatoes, chopped
1 pinch Himalayan salt
2 handfuls of spinach, separated (approximately 2 cups firmly packed)

1. Place cashews in food processor. Add lemon juice and olive oil. Process until smooth.
2. Add shallot and garlic. Process until well blended.
3. Add 1 handful of the spinach. Continue to process until spinach is well incorporated.
4. Remove the mixture from the food processor. Hand chop the remaining handful of spinach and stir in. You will have more than you need for the quiche. It is great on crackers.

Filling

¾ cup Spinach Cashew Cheese Spread
1 cup cherry tomatoes, halved
1 cup pea pods, chopped into ½-inch pieces
½ cup sun-dried tomatoes, softened and chopped

1. Mix together all ingredients and place in prepared quiche crust.
2. Refrigerate at least a couple of hours to set up.

Potato Pancakes with Apple Sauce

⅓ cup pine nuts, ground fine
1 clove garlic
1 large potato, grated (I used a red potato)
water
1 tablespoon Himalayan salt
½ purple onion
2 tablespoons dried rosemary
1 tablespoon olive oil

1. Put pine nuts in food processor and pulse until fine. Set aside.
2. With food processor running, drop in clove of garlic.
3. Switch blades and grate potato.
4. Put potato and garlic in a bowl filled with water and salt, let soak for 10 minutes, drain.
5. Meanwhile, chop the onion.
6. Combine drained potato and garlic mixture, onion, pine nuts, rosemary, and olive oil. Place on dehydrator screens in pancake shapes, about 4 inches across. Dehydrate at 145 degrees for 45 minutes, then reduce heat and finish dehydrating at 115 degrees for 2 more hours. You want them to be fully dry. Remove with spatula and serve with raw Apple Sauce.

Apple Sauce

4 apples, cored
2 tablespoons agave nectar(optional)
½ teaspoon cinnamon

1. Place all ingredients in the food processor. Process untill you achieve applesauce consistency.

Savory Zucchini Wraps with Squash, Craisins, and Sage Cream

Squash and sage are a great combination. Throw in a few dried cranberries for an accent and you have a dish that's both easy to make and worthy of company. By soaking the squash beforehand and placing it in the dehydrator in the morning, the starches are reduced and your warm squash is ready to go.

For this recipe, I used carnival squash. They are sweet, full of beta-carotene (which is an anti-oxidant and anti-inflammatory), vitamins A and C, and fiber. Other benefits include folate, copper, vitamin B6, niacin, and omega-3 fatty acids.

This recipe might seem a little complicated at first but it is actually very easy. Read through it first. You have a little advanced preparation but only minutes of actual food handling and very few ingredients. Enjoy!

Dehydrated Squash

SERVES 4

2 medium carnival or acorn squash
2 tablespoons olive oil
Himalayan salt and pepper, to taste

1. The night before: Peel and cube squash and place in cold, salted water. Place in refrigerator over night.
2. In the morning, drain, toss with olive oil, salt, and pepper. Place on screens in dehydrator. Dehydrate at 115 degrees for 8 hours.

Continued…

Zucchini Wraps

4 cups zucchini, *pureed*
1 cup flax seeds, *ground*
2 tablespoons olive oil
2 tablespoons fine herbs

1. Combine all ingredients. Spread on nonstick sheet. You may need two sheets. You want this to be at least ¼ inch thick as zucchini will greatly reduce when dehydrated.
2. Place in dehydrator with squash. You will want to peel the sheet off half way through the dehydration. Always place face up after you remove the sheet. They should be dried but not crisp.
3. Dehydration time will be around 8 hours at 115. Cut into quarters. Makes 4–5 wraps.

Sage "Cream" Sauce

1 cup cashews, *soaked overnight, rinsed, and drained*
½ cup pine nuts
2 tablespoons olive oil
½ lemon, *juice from*
2 tablespoons dried sage
Himalayan salt and pepper, to taste

1. Place all ingredients in food processor and process until well blended and smooth. You can also put this in the high-speed blender for an even smoother consistency.

Assembly

½ cup dried cranberries
Sage Cream Sauce
Zucchini Wraps
Dehydrated Squash

1. Spread Sage Cream Sauce on wrap. Top with squash and dried cranberries. Roll, cut, and enjoy!

Sun-Dried Tomato and Veggie "Pasta"

Marinated Mushrooms

SERVES 4

2 cups mushrooms, sliced
3 tablespoons Nama Shoyu
3 tablespoons olive oil
1 tablespoon agave nectar (optional)

1. Mix together Nama Shoyu, olive oil, and agave, if desired.
2. Pour over mushrooms, stir to combine. Let sit to marinate for at least 3–4 hours in the refrigerator. I prefer overnight.

Sauce

½ cup Sun-Dried Tomato Spread (see page 36)
¼ cup filtered water
1 cup pea pods, chopped
¼ cup sun-dried tomatoes, chopped
2 scallions, thinly sliced
2 yellow squash

1. Add water to sauce, whisk to thin out.
2. Add chopped veggies and mix together. Make noodles from yellow squash with spiralizer or by thinly slicing. Top noodles with sauce.

Stuffed Avocados with Chipotle "Mayo"

MAKES 6

3 avocados
1 cup jicama, diced
½ cup celery, diced
1 ½ cups cherry tomatoes, chopped
1 cup sunflower seeds
½ cup sweet onion, diced

1. Make Chipotle Mayo (see page 58 for recipe) and set aside.
2. Slice avocados in half, remove pit, and set aside.
3. Combine diced jicama, celery, cherry tomatoes, sunflower seeds, and chopped onion.
4. Stir in ½–1 cup of the Chipotle Mayo.
5. Spoon into avocado halves.

Cauliflower Steaks

*L*ooking for a great raw food dinner that is perfect for a summer evening? With just a little prep time, you can serve your family or friends these delicious, 100 percent raw "steaks"! Starting your prep early in the day, a few simple steps, into the dehydrator, and you don't have to worry about it until dinner! Enjoy!

2 cauliflower heads
2 tablespoons agave nectar
½ cup olive oil, cold pressed
¼ cup Nama Shoyu

1. Slice cauliflower into ½-inch slices and place in glass pan.
2. Blend together agave, olive oil, and Nama Shoyu.
3. Pour marinade over cauliflower steaks. (You will have some cauliflower that breaks off... just marinate that, too), flip to coat.
4. Marinate for at least 1 hour in the refrigerator.
5. Dehydrate on screens for 30 minutes at 145 degrees, then reduce heat to 115 degrees and finish dehydrating for 4–5 hours.

Spinach Cashew Zucchini "Pasta"

SERVES 2-4

2 medium zucchini
¾ cup mushrooms, marinated (see page 161)
1 cup cherry tomatoes, halved
1 cup pea pods, chopped
5 scallions, sliced
½ cup sun-dried tomatoes, chopped
½ cup Spinach Cashew Cheese Spread (see page 144)
¼ cup water
Himalayan salt and pepper, to taste

1. Make zucchini noodles with spiral cutter.
2. Mix together all ingredients except Spinach Cashew Cheese Spread.
3. Add water to spread. Mix to thin.
4. Add to veggie mixture. Mix well.

Spinach Mushroom Tarts

I remember getting grounded for playing with my food. Seriously. I was crushing crackers and making little designs in my soup. It sent my dad right over the edge. I don't think he would be so upset anymore. Actually, I think he would be downright pleased. I believe that eating raw food should not be boring or difficult. It should be a fun culinary adventure. If I see a recipe that has 40 ingredients, I'm not likely to try it. I am a bit lazy when it comes to working in the kitchen.

The challenge I give to myself is to make tasty, beautiful creations without too much fuss. I want the food to be approachable and easy! You can throw this little beauty together in minutes with just a little advanced prep. Have fun go and play with your food!

Mushrooms

2 cups mushrooms, sliced (I use a mix of different varieties)
⅓ cup olive oil
⅓ cup balsamic vinegar
1 tablespoon raw honey or agave nectar (optional)

1. Whisk together olive oil, balsamic vinegar, and honey or agave.
2. Place mushrooms in a bowl, pour marinade over mushrooms. Cover and let sit over night in the refrigerator. You can stir occasionally to make sure you get good distribution.

Continued...

Crust

1 cup soaked almonds, soaked overnight and drained
1 cup hazelnuts
½ cup brown flax seeds
pinch Himalayan salt
pepper, to taste

1. Place almonds in food processor with hazelnuts, flax seeds, salt, and pepper. Process until a coarse-meal texture is achieved.
2. Place enough in ring to make a layer about ⅓ inch thick. You want to pack it in tightly. If you are using a pie plate, make a crust about ⅓ inch thick.
3. Place in dehydrator for 1–2 hours at 115 degrees. Cool.

Filling

2 cups cashews, soaked overnight, rinsed, and drained
½ lemon, juice from
1 clove garlic, roughly chopped
3 tablespoons shallots, roughly chopped
pinch Himalayan salt
1 cup marinated mushrooms, drained
½ cup spinach, wilted by rubbing between hands (Save a little for topping)

1. You will be making the filling in two steps. Begin by placing the cashews, lemon juice, garlic, shallots, and salt in the food processor. Process until smooth.
2. Remove from food processor, mix in 1 cup of the mushrooms.
3. Halve the mixture and place in two separate bowls.
4. To the second bowl, add the wilted spinach

Assembly

1. Get your crust. Your first layer will be the mushroom filling without spinach. Make this layer about 1 inch thick. Pat it in.
2. Second layer will be the mixture with the spinach. Refrigerate for at least 1 hour.
3. Unmold if you are using the rings. Top with additional mushrooms and spinach.

Stuffed Mushrooms

4 cups mushrooms, divided
¼ cup olive oil
¼ cup + 2 tablespoons Nama Shoyu, divided
1 tablespoon agave nectar (optional)
1 cup pumpkin seeds, soaked for 3 hours and drained
1 cup sunflower seeds, soaked for 3 hours and drained
1 tablespoon water
1 clove garlic
1 shallot
¼ cup parsley
1 tablespoon tarragon
1 tablespoon thyme
pinch Himalayan salt
pinch pepper

Marinated Mushrooms

1. Remove the stems and gills from 2 cups of the mushrooms.
2. Combine Nama Shoyu, olive oil, and agave.
3. Place mushrooms and marinade in bowl, coat to combine. Let sit, stirring occasionally for at least 3 hours. I like to marinate overnight.

Filling

1. Finely chop garlic and shallot in food processor. Remove to bowl.
2. Place 2 cups mushrooms in food processor. Pulse until they are finely chopped. Put in bowl with garlic and shallots.
3. Process sunflower seeds and pumpkin seeds in food processor until a paste consistency is achieved. Add to bowl.
4. Stir in remaining ingredients, spoon into drained, marinated mushroom tops. Sprinkle tops with more tarragon.

Tomato Napoleon with Basil Cashew Cheese and Basil Oil

*F*ood inspires me. Working with the ingredients, smelling them, tasting them, trying to guess what will go with what. I am amazed at how you can have an idea, start throwing some things together, and, within a matter of minutes, transform the familiar into something completely new yet wonderful. It is a transition from the unknown to the known. Plus we get to eat it!

This little tomato Napoleon is quite simple but delicious. A quick and easy basil cashew cheese is combined with the layers of tomato and zucchini. It is a great end of summer treat.

Basil Cashew Cheese Spread

1 cup cashews, soaked overnight, rinsed, and drained
2 tablespoons lemon juice
1 clove garlic
pinch Himalayan salt
1 cup basil leaves

1. Start food processor. Drop garlic into processor and run until chopped.
2. Add cashews, lemon juice, and salt and process until smooth (it will be a little grainy).
3. Add basil and pulse until basil is chopped up and combined into cheese.

Continued...

Tomato Napoleon continued...

Assembly:

1 small tomato
2 slices zucchini (the same size as the tomato)
Basil Cashew Cheese Spread
Basil Oil (see page 121)

1. Cut the tomato in thirds.
2. Form a patty of the Basil Cashew Cheese Spread the same size as the tomato slice.
3. Layer tomato slice, zucchini, and cheese, repeat. Drizzle Basil Oil over top. You can also add balsamic vinegar (highly recommended).

main dishes

Marinated Mushrooms and Mashed Rosemary Cauliflower

SERVES 2–4

Mushrooms:

3 large portobello mushrooms, sliced ⅓ inch thick
⅓ cup olive oil
⅓ cup Nama Shoyu
1 tablespoon agave nectar

1. Mix marinade ingredients, pour over mushrooms, and marinate for at least 4 hours. I like to do this the night before and leave them in the refrigerator. You will need to occasionally stir them.

Cauliflower Mash

1 large head cauliflower
olive oil
Himalayan salt and pepper
⅓ cup pine nuts
1 teaspoon rosemary, coarsely chopped
1 tablespoon olive oil
2 tablespoons water

1. Cut all florets off of the main stem. Thinly slice.
2. Place slices (and any extra pieces) in bowl. Sprinkle with oil, salt, and pepper. Toss.
3. Place on two nonstick dehydrator sheets and spread so there is just one layer of cauliflower. Dehydrate at 115 degrees for 2 hours.
4. Place in food processor along with pine nuts, oil, and water. Process until pureed.
5. Add rosemary and blend. Salt and pepper to taste. I love to warm this up in the dehydrator before serving.

main dishes   161

Walnut Basil Pesto Cream with Veggies

*T*raditional pesto is made from basil, pine nuts, olive oil, garlic, and Parmesan cheese. We can still use the basil, olive oil, and garlic, but since pine nuts have become insanely expensive and Parmesan cheese doesn't fit the bill for a raw food recipe, I decided to take a stab at walnut pesto! As you know, walnuts are packed with nutrition, and pesto is just yummy. You can serve this over veggie noodles, spoon it on tomatoes, turn it into a dip, put it on raw pizza, and incorporate it in many other raw recipes.

Pesto is bursting with the flavor of basil and garlic. It freezes well and can quickly convert the simplest veggies into a great meal that is savory and delicious. It is a great way to use and store your basil.

Walnut Basil Pesto

MAKES 1 ½ CUPS

2 cup basil leaves, packed
½ cup walnuts
½ cup olive oil
2 cloves garlic
squeeze of lemon juice

1. With food processor running, drop in two cloves of garlic.
2. Stop machine and add basil and walnuts. Pulse until well chopped.
3. Add olive oil and lemon juice and pulse until well combined.

*Chef's Note: I love garlic and have loaded this pesto with it. You can definitely cut back if you wish. To freeze, place in ice cube trays, freeze, then move to storage container and keep in freezer.

Walnut Basil Pesto Cream Sauce

MAKES 1 CUP

1 cup cashews, soaked overnight, rinsed, and drained
¾ cup filtered water
5 tablespoons Basil Walnut Pesto, divided

1. In high-speed blender, blend cashews and water until smooth.
2. Add 2 tablespoons of the Basil Walnut Pesto and blend well.
3. Remove to bowl and stir in 3 more tablespoons of the Basil Walnut Pesto.

Basil Walnut Pesto Cream with Veggies

SERVES 2–4

1 cup Basil Walnut Pesto Cream
2 medium zucchinis
1 cup cherry tomatoes, halved
1 cup mushrooms, sliced
¼ cup pine nuts (optional)

1. Put the zucchinis through the spiralizer to make noodles.
2. Toss together zucchini noodles, tomatoes, mushrooms, and ½ –1 cup of the Basil Walnut Pesto Cream.
3. Top with pine nuts and serve.

Zucchini Corn Cakes with Cilantro Cream

Corn Cakes

SERVES 4

2 cups shredded zucchini (approximately 2 medium zucchinis)
4 ears fresh corn
1 clove garlic
½ teaspoon dried mustard
⅛ teaspoon white pepper
pinch Himalayan salt
½ cup flax seeds, ground fine

1. Place grated zucchini in bowl, set aside.
2. With a sharp knife, cut kernels off of the ears of corn. Set 2 cups aside. Place remaining 2 cups in food processor.
3. Add garlic, dried mustard, white pepper, and pinch of salt to the food processor. Process until corn turns to a liquid mash.
4. Add ground flax seeds and pulse until combined. Do not over-mix.
5. Add to zucchini along with the remaining 2 cups of corn.
6. Shape into patties about ½ inch thick and 4 inches across. Place on nonstick sheets.

Continued...

Zucchini Corn Cakes with Cilantro Cream continued...

7. Dehydrate for 1 hour at 145 degrees, transfer to screens and reduce heat to 115 degrees and dehydrate for 5–6 hours. The outside should be crispy but the insides still a little moist.
8. Top with Cilantro Cream.

Cilantro Cream

1 cup cashews, soaked until soft
½ cup young Thai coconut flesh
2–3 tablespoons coconut water, from young coconut
1 small garlic clove
pinch Himalayan salt
pinch pepper
2 teaspoons fresh cilantro, chopped fine

1. Combine cashews, coconut, coconut water, garlic, salt, and pepper in high-speed blender.
2. Blend until very smooth.
3. Stir in chopped cilantro by hand.

Mushroom Leek Tart

2 cups sliced mushrooms
⅓ cup olive oil
3 tablespoons Nama Shoyu
2 cups spinach
1 ½ cup leeks, thinly sliced
1 ½ cup cashews
1 ½ cup water
2 teaspoons tarragon
1 teaspoon white pepper
pinch Himalayan salt

1. The night before: Combine mushrooms, olive oil, and Nama Shoyu. Mix well, place in refrigerator to marinate.
2. Wrap foil around the outside of a 10-inch tart pan. You are doing this to prevent leakage. Oil inside.
3. Rinse marinated mushrooms and spread in the bottom of a prepared tart pan.
4. Crush spinach between hands and spread on top of the mushrooms.
5. Spread leeks on top of the spinach.
6. In high-speed blender, combine cashews, water, tarragon, pepper, and salt. Blend until smooth.
7. Pour over veggies in tart pan.
8. Place in dehydrator. Dehydrate at 145 degrees for 1 hour, reduce heat, and continue dehydrating at 115 degrees for another 9 hours.

Raw Vegan Sushi

SERVES 2–4

$\mathcal{I}$ love sushi. The first time I ate it I was surprised by the explosion of flavor that hit my tongue. It was so different from anything that I had ever eaten! The refreshing and interesting combination of flavors inspired me to create a raw version. Even though sushi is thought to be raw because of the fish, it contains cooked rice. Plus, most raw recipes are also vegan, so eating fish is not in the cards.

The challenge was to create a raw food recipe that would replace the rice but still have approximately the same texture. I ended up sprouting kamut, a wonderful grain that is full of protein and goodness. Processing it in the food processor gave it the texture that it needed to hold together. A sushi mat is needed to make this, but they are quite easy to use.

1 large portobello mushroom
2 tablespoons Nama Shoyu
2 tablespoons olive oil
1 tablespoon toasted sesame oil
½ sunflower sprouts
2 carrots
½ cucumber
2 cups sprouted kamut
1 avocado, sliced
2 seaweed sheets

1. Cut the portobello mushroom into slices about ¼ to ½ inch thick. Toss with Nama Shoyu and olive oil and let sit for at least 30 minutes.
2. Afterwards, process the kamut, Nama Shoyu, and toasted sesame oil in a food processor until the kamut starts to break apart. Set aside.
3. Slice carrots and cucumber into match stick pieces, slice the avocado into ¼-inch pieces. Set aside.
4. Lay your sheet of seaweed on the sushi mat. Spread half the sheet with the kamut mixture. Place the avocado, carrots, cucumber, sunflower sprouts and mushrooms on top of the kamut.
5. Using the mat, carefully and tightly, roll the seaweed into a sushi roll. Cut with a serrated knife.

desserts

Apple Cranberry "Cheesecake"

I needed to come up with a menu for a raw food dessert class, so I decided to whip up a "cheesecake" recipe. It was actually pretty easy. And taste? The class was blown away. The crust is almonds and dates, and the base of the "cheesecake" is cashews! Don't worry, I added apples and dried cranberries for that hint of fruit. The result? A healthy, tasty dessert that would be completely at home on your Thanksgiving or holiday table. The consensus of the class was that nonraw people would never guess that this is raw, vegan, or healthy!

Don't be intimidated by this one, 1 serving is equivalent to only eating ¼ cup cashews and ⅛ cup of almonds! Cashews are a good source of protein, fiber, and also potassium, B vitamin, foliate, magnesium, phosphorous, selenium, and copper.

SERVES 6-8

Crust

1 cup almonds
4 pitted dates, soaked until soft

1. Combine almonds and dates in food processor until fine crumb is achieved.
2. Set aside ⅓ cup for topping.
3. Pack into 6-inch spring form pan and refrigerate.

Continued…

Topping

3 apples, peeled and sliced thinly
¼ cup agave nectar
½ teaspoon cinnamon
⅓ cup dried cranberries
2 tablespoons coconut butter, softened
⅓ cup crust

1. Combine apples, agave, and cinnamon.
2. Place on nonstick dehydrator sheet and dehydrate at 115 degrees for 2 hours, stirring once during dehydration.

Filling

2 cups cashews, soaked overnight, rinsed, and drained
1 teaspoon lemon juice
½ cup coconut butter, softened
¼ cup agave nectar
1 teaspoon vanilla
1 teaspoon cinnamon
¼ teaspoon ground cloves
¼ teaspoon nutmeg

1. Combine all ingredients in food processor. Process until smooth.
2. Pour over crust and place in refrigerator.

Assembly

1. Combine topping with the ⅓ cup crust that you have set aside.
2. Sprinkle on top of "cheesecake."
3. Refrigerate at least 3 hours or until set.

Cacao Mint Macaroons

2 cups dried coconut, unsweetened
¼ cup mint leaves
½ cup almonds
¼ cup maple syrup
¼ cup agave nectar
¼ cup coconut oil, melted

1. Place mint leaves and almonds in food processor (I used pre-soaked, dehydrated almonds). Process until ground fine.
2. Whisk together maple syrup, agave, and coconut oil.
3. Mix together coconut, almond mint mixture, and agave mixture.
4. Take a tablespoon and dip into hot water, pack with mixture, and then turn out onto mesh dehydrator sheet.
5. Dehydrate for 6+ hours or until desired dryness is achieved. You can start the dehydration at 145 degrees for the first hour, then reduce to 115 degrees.
6. Cool.
7. Dip in cacao coating and chill.

Cacao Coating

½ cup cacao powder
¼ cup maple syrup
¼ cup agave nectar
¼ cup coconut oil, melted
½ teaspoon vanilla
pinch Himalayan salt

1. Whisk all ingredients together.
2. Dip macaroons into cacao mixture and chill. You can let the cacao mixture cool a little before dipping for a thicker coating.

Cacao Ganache Raspberry Tart

Want a quick, beautiful, gourmet raw food dessert recipe that tastes like heaven? Throw together this little tart and your guests will be impressed. Start with a quick ganache, throw in some raspberries and a little nut crust, and within minutes, you have this beautiful dessert.

Crust

MAKES 1 10-INCH TART

½ cup almonds, ground fine
2 tablespoons cacao powder
1 tablespoon coconut butter or coconut oil, softened
1 tablespoon agave nectar

1. Combine all ingredients.

Ganache

½ cup cacao powder
½ cup agave nectar
¼ cup coconut butter, softened

1. Whisk together all ingredients.

Assembly

1 pint raspberries
Crust
Ganache

1. Pat crust into 10-inch ring mold to make a crust ¼ inch thick. Press hard to make solid.
2. Top with a thin layer of the Ganache. Top the Ganache with a layer of raspberries, then fill with Ganache to ½ inch from top of mold. Top with raspberries.
3. Refrigerate until firm and carefully unmold, pushing up from the bottom.

Raw Apple Pie with Maple-Cinnamon Glaze

Crust

2 cups walnuts, soaked until soft
2 tablespoons coconut butter, softened
1 tablespoon agave nectar

1. Drain walnuts. Place in food processor and process until a coarse meal is achieved.
2. Add coconut butter and agave. Mix until well combined.
3. Press ¼ inch thick into tart shells or 9-inch pie plate.
4. Dehydrate for 3 hours at 115 degrees. You can start at 145 degrees for 45 minutes and then lower the temperature for quicker dehydration.

Filling

4 apples, peeled, cored, and thinly sliced
1/2 lemon, juice from
¼ cup maple syrup
¼ cup agave nectar
1 teaspoon cinnamon
⅓ cup raw oat flour

1. Place apple slices in bowl.
2. Sprinkle with lemon juice and toss.

Continued...

3. Mix together maple syrup, agave, and cinnamon.
4. Stir into apple mixture.
5. Add oat flour and toss to coat.
6. Place filling in two separate glass pie plates.
7. Place in dehydrator for 6 hours, stirring occasionally. Add water if mixture starts to dry out.

Maple-Cinnamon Glaze

1 tablespoon coconut butter, softened
3 tablespoons maple syrup
½ teaspoon cinnamon

1. Whisk all ingredients together to combine.

Assembly

1. Place filling in 4 4-inch tart shells or one 1-inch pie plate that you have already prepared with the crust.
2. Place back into dehydrator for 2 hours.
3. Remove and top with Maple-Cinnamon Glaze.

Cacao Cinnamon-Pecan Whoopie Pies

I was walking past a store one day and they had whoopie pies in their window. Of course the first thing I thought was, "I need a raw food version of those!" I got home and set to work, coming up with a cinnamon-pecan filling instead of the traditional vanilla one. Full of nutritious ingredients, these make a wonderful treat or dessert. The filling is fast and easy and the actual cookies are not too difficult either. They do require rolling out and dehydrating, so leave time for that.

Cookies

MAKES ONE DOZEN

2 cups oat flour
½ cup cacao powder
¼ cup coconut butter, softened
¼ cup agave nectar
¼ cup maple syrup

1. Place all dry ingredients in food processor. Pulse to combine.
2. Whisk together wet ingredients. Add to dry and process until very well combined. If needed, you can add 1 tablespoon of water.
3. Flatten out to a disk shape on nonstick dehydrator sheet. Cover top with wax or parchment paper and roll out to ¼ inch thick. You can pat these into shapes also, but the dough is really sticky.
4. Cut with a ring cutter. Peel away extra dough leaving circles on tray. Repeat until you have used up the dough.
5. Place in dehydrator at 115 degrees for 4 hours. Peel off of nonstick sheet and dehydrate 2–4 more hours. These should be dry but not brittle. A little softness should remain.

Continued…

Cacao Cinnamon-Pecan Whoopie Pies continued...

Filling

2 cups pecans, soaked and drained
¼ cup agave nectar
⅓ cup coconut butter, softened
1 teaspoon cinnamon

1.   Mix all ingredients in food processor until very well combined.
     Use for filling between 2 cookies.

Almond Cherry Macaroons

MAKES APPROXIMATELY 2 DOZEN

2 cups dried coconut, unsweetened
½ cup almonds
½ cup dried cherries, chopped
½ cup agave nectar
¼ cup coconut oil, softened
1 teaspoon almond extract

1. Place almonds in food processor and process until a coarse meal texture is achieved.
2. Add coconut, dried cherries, coconut oil, agave, and extract. Process until mixture starts to hold together.
3. I use a tablespoon to scoop the mixture out and press into a ball. Place on dehydrator sheets and dehydrate at 115 degrees until desired consistency is achieved (8–10 hours). I like them dry on the outside but still a little soft on the inside.

Banana Cream Tart with Walnut Crust

Crust

1 ½ cup walnuts
1 cup Brazil nuts
5 dates, soaked until soft
2 tablespoons coconut butter, softened

1. Pulse walnuts and Brazil nuts in food processor until coarsely chopped.
2. Chop dates and add to food processor with coconut butter. Process until well blended.
3. Press into two 4-inch tart shells. Crust should be ¼ inch thick all around.

Filling

2 cups cashews, soaked overnight, rinsed and drained
1 cup young Thai coconut flesh
¼ cup coconut water, from young coconut
¼ cup coconut butter, softened
1 teaspoon lemon juice
¼ cup agave nectar
1 vanilla bean
2 bananas, sliced and separated

1. Process cashews, young coconut flesh, and coconut water in food processor until well blended.
2. Add lemon juice, agave, coconut butter, and 1 banana and continue to process until light, fluffy, and very well processed.
3. Transfer to bowl and add second sliced banana, stir to combine.
4. Refrigerate for 30 minutes. Remove from refrigerator, spoon into crusts, and sprinkle with leftover crust mixture and dried coconut. Top with melted Raw Chocolate.

Raw Chocolate

(see page 91)

Cacao and Vanilla Banana-Walnut Crepes

*O*ne of my favorite things to do when experimenting with new recipes is to make my "former" favorite foods in a raw version. I love crepes. My daughters and I enjoyed many Sunday mornings with a plate of crepes. But the old version with eggs, flour, sugar, etc., leave me feeling tired, bloated, and nutritionally devoid!

I wanted to make a truly gourmet crepe that would qualify as a raw food dessert. My other name for these is tuxedo crepes because they are black and white—compliments of the cacao cream and the vanilla cream fillings! I added ground walnuts to the banana crepes not only for nutritional value, but also to provide a great texture. Make sure you don't overdehydrate the crepes or you will have fruit leather!

Crepes

5 ripe bananas
½ cup walnuts, ground

1. Place bananas in food processor. Process until liquid.
2. Add ground walnuts and pulse to combine.
3. Spoon into 5-inch circles on your nonstick sheets. Dehydrate at 115 degrees about 8 hours. You want these to be very pliable. If you over dehydrate, they will be too chewy.

Continued…

Cashew Vanilla Cream

1 young Thai coconut, flesh from (approximately 3/4 cup)
½ cup cashews, soaked overnight, rinsed, and drained
splash of Madagascar vanilla
pulp from 1 vanilla bean

1. Place the cashews in high-speed blender. Blend.
2. Add the coconut meat and vanilla. Process until well blended. You can refrigerate to thicken if needed.

Chocolate (Cacao) Cinnamon Cream

¾ cup pitted dates, soaked until very soft
2 avocados
1 ½ cups almond milk
½ cup almond butter
¾ cup cacao powder
½ cup agave nectar
1 tablespoon cinnamon

1. In food processor or blender, combine all ingredients and blend or process until smooth. Refrigerate.

Assembly

2 fresh bananas
Cashew Vanilla Cream
Cacao Cinnamon Cream

1. Slice fresh bananas.
2. Place 1 crepe on plate, top with a layer of Cacao Cinnamon Cream.
3. Layer with fresh sliced bananas.
4. Place another crepe on top of the bananas, spread Cashew Vanilla cream on crepe, top with more sliced bananas and top with third crepe. These are very yummy, beautiful, and good for you!

Cacao Walnut Cookies

2 cups almond flour
½ cup flax seeds, ground
½ cup cacao powder
⅓ cup olive oil
⅓ cup water
⅓ cup agave nectar
1 tablespoon vanilla
1 cup chopped walnuts

1. Mix almond flour, flax, and cacao powder.
2. Stir in oil, water, agave, and vanilla.
3. When it is well mixed, stir in chopped walnuts.
4. Form into balls, press flat with palms, and place on dehydrator screens.
5. Dehydrate 1 hour at 145 degrees, then reduce to 115 degrees and dehydrate for at least 5 hours or until desired dryness is achieved.

Cacao Walnut Macaroons

2 cups dried coconut, unsweetened
½ cup almond flour
⅓ cup cacao powder
¼ cup coconut butter, softened
¼ cup maple syrup
¼ cup agave nectar
1 vanilla bean, scrapings from inside
1 cup walnuts, chopped

1. Mix all ingredients except walnuts until very well combined.
2. Stir in walnuts.
3. Shape into balls and dehydrate at 115 degrees for 4–5 hours.

Chocolate Chocolate Chip Cookies

1 cup pureed zucchini
⅓ cup agave nectar
½ cup coconut butter, softened
1 cup raw oat flour
1 ½ cups raw flaked oats
½ cup cacao powder
½ teaspoon cinnamon
½ cup chopped walnuts (optional)
½ cup cacao nibs (optional)

1. Combine zucchini puree (simply puree zucchini in your food processor), agave, and coconut butter in food processor. Blend well.
2. Mix together oat flour, cacao powder, and cinnamon.
3. Stir in wet mixture. Combine well.
4. Stir in oats, optional walnuts, and optional cacao nibs. Mix well.
5. Press into cookie shapes and dehydrate for 30 minutes at 145 degrees, reduce heat, and dehydrate for 4–5 more hours at 115 degrees.

Cinnamon Oatmeal Raisin Cookies

2 cups raw flaked oats
1 cup raw oat flour
1 cup apple puree (about 3 medium apples)
½ cup coconut oil, softened
¼ cup agave nectar
1 teaspoon cinnamon
1 cup raisins

1. To make the apple puree: Quarter and core apples. Leave the peel on. Place in food processor and process until pureed.
2. Place oats and oat flour in bowl. Mix together.
3. Mix in remaining ingredients in order.
4. Drop in mounds on nonstick sheets. Flatten slightly.
5. Place in dehydrator for 45 minutes at 145 degrees, remove from nonstick sheets, and place on screen. Continue dehydrating at 115 degrees for 6–8 hours or until almost dry.

Cacao Walnut Fudge

Almond Butter

MAKES 1 CUP

2 cups almonds

1. Place almonds in food processor. Process, scraping down the sides of the bowl as needed.
2. It will take anywhere from 6–12 minutes for the butter to form. You will go through a few stages: first a coarse meal, second it will ball up, third it will start to spread out, and finally, after the correct amount of time, you will see the oils have released and the butter is shiny. Be patient. The butter heats up but never gets over 100 degrees.

Cacao Walnut Fudge

1 cup Almond Butter
½ cup cacao powder
¼ cup agave nectar
½ cup walnuts, chopped

1. Mix together Almond Butter, cacao powder, and agave. It is easiest to do this with your hand.
2. Once it is well combined, mix in the walnuts.
3. You can put this in an 8 x 8-inch square pan or, use a mold. Refrigerate for at least 2 hours.

Chocolate Mousse

$\mathscr{C}$hocolate, affectionately called food of the gods, comes from the cacao tree. Beautiful yellow-green pods hang from the tree's trunk and branches. When cut open, the edible, fibrous white pulp is sought after by people native to the area. Embedded in the pulp are dark purple seeds that, after being dried and processed, become "chocolate beans." When eating a raw food diet, we are not interested in the processed chocolate that has lost many of its nutrients; we are interested in chocolate in its raw form: cacao.

Cacao has a high level of antioxidants, and is an excellent source of dietary fiber. It is one of the highest dietary sources of magnesium, and contains an impressively high iron content. It also has many other essential minerals in significant quantities. Cacao is a source of serotonin, dopamine, and phenylethylamine, which can help alleviate depression and increase feelings of well-being. Cacao also contains anandamide, which delivers feelings of bliss, and B vitamins, which are essential to brain health.

As you enjoy this chocolate mousse, made with cacao and other healthy ingredients, know that you are not only experiencing bliss on your palate, but are also doing your brain, body, and attitude a favor.

¾ cup pitted dates, soaked until very soft
2 avocados
1 cup almond milk
½ cup almond butter
¾ cup cacao powder
½ cup agave nectar

1. In food processor or blender, combine all ingredients and blend or process until smooth.
2. Refrigerate, then enjoy. You will not believe how good this is!

Cinnamon and Fruit Chia Pudding

MAKES 4 SERVINGS

Cashew Cream

2 cups cashews, soaked overnight
2 cups filtered water

1. Drain and rinse cashews.
2. Combine with filtered water in blender (I used a high-speed blender) and blend until smooth.
3. Refrigerate.

Pudding

1 ¾ cups Cashew Cream
½ cup chia seeds
½ cup agave nectar
1 teaspoon vanilla
1 teaspoon cinnamon
1 cup strawberries, sliced
1 cup blueberries

1. Mix together Cashew Cream, chia seeds, agave, vanilla, and cinnamon. Set aside.
2. Slice strawberries.
3. When chia pudding has thickened up (about 5–10 minutes) stir in sliced strawberries and blueberries.
4. Keep refrigerated.

Cinnamon Plum Sorbet

2 cups plum puree (the insides)
½ cup agave nectar
1 cup Almond Milk
½ teaspoon cinnamon
pinch salt

1. Place all ingredients in blender and blend until smooth.
2. Pour into ice cream freezer and freeze according to manufacturer's instructions.

Almond Milk

1 cup almonds, soaked overnight, rinsed, and drained
4 cups filtered water
2 dates
1 vanilla bean

1. Add almonds to high-speed blender with the filtered water, dates, and vanilla bean.
2. Process for 2 minutes. Strain through nut-milk bag. You can save the remaining pulp, dehydrate it, and use it as flour for other recipes.

Cacao Coconut Ganache Tart

MAKES 4–6 SERVINGS

Crust

1 cup dried coconut, unsweetened
⅓ cup coconut oil, melted
½ cup almonds, soaked overnight, rinsed, and drained

1. Combine all ingredients in food processor.
2. Pat into two 4-inch tart pans and refrigerate.

Filling

½ cup cacao powder
½ cup agave nectar
¼ cup coconut oil, melted

1. Melt coconut oil over hot water or in the dehydrator.
2. Whisk together cacao powder, coconut oil, and agave.
3. Pour into tart shells and refrigerate for at least 30 minutes.

Cinnamon Ginger Truffles

Truffles

MAKES ABOUT 2 DOZEN

2 cups almonds, ground fine
1 tablesoon cinnamon
1 teaspoon ginger
½ teaspoon nutmeg
¼ teaspoon cloves
½ cup agave nectar
½ cup dried cranberries
½ cup golden raisins
dried coconut (optional)
cacao powder (optional)

1. Place almonds in food processor and process until finely ground.
2. Add spices and combine.
3. Add cranberries and raisins. Process for 5 seconds.
4. Add agave and process until well blended.
5. Roll into balls. This is sticky, so wetting your hands will help. If desired, roll in dried coconut or cacao powder for more alternatives.

Cranberry Pecan Torte

Wanting a fun and festive recipe for a raw dessert class, I came up with the idea for this torte. What could be more festive than cranberries during the holidays? I wanted to teach people the basics so they could branhch off and use what they learned to make their own recipes!

We started with a cashew cream. I showed them how to turn that into a chia seed pudding, and then cashew whipping cream. From there, we made a basic nut crust that, when combined with the cashew whipped cream and filling ingredients, became a cranberry pecan torte. Topped off with a great chocolate ganache, the class was thrilled with the tasty results! You will be amazed at how easy this is to throw together, and how much your family and friends will love it!

Chocolate Crust

MAKES 1 TEN-INCH TORTE

2 cups almonds, finely ground*
¼ cup cacao powder
¼ cup coconut oil, melted

1. Mix together almonds, cacao powder and coconut oil. Pat in tart shell.

*I used almonds that had been presoaked and dried in the dehydrator.

Filling

2 cups cashews, soaked
1 ½ cups filtered water
1 ½ cups coconut oil, melted
½ cup agave nectar
1 cup fresh cranberries, chopped
¾ cup pecans, chopped

1. In high-speed blender, combine cashews and water. Blend until smooth.
2. Blend in coconut oil and agave.
3. Remove to bowl and stir in cranberries and pecans.
4. Pour into crust. Refrigerate until set. This will take several hours; you may want to make this the night before.
5. Top with ganache.

Ganache

½ cup cacao powder
½ cup agave nectar
¼ cup coconut oil, melted

1. Whisk all ingredients together.

Dried Cherry Chocolate Truffles

MAKES 30

1 cup Almond Butter (see page 194)
½ cup cacao powder
¼ cup agave nectar
30 dried cherries

1. Mix all ingredients except cherries in food processor.
2. Form a small disk, place dried cherry in the middle, and wrap disk around the cherry. Roll into ball. Refrigerate.

Halvah

1 ½ cups sesame seeds
3 tablespoons coconut butter, softened
½ cup dried coconut, unsweetened
⅓ cup honey
Ganache (see page 203)

1. Mix together all ingredients except Ganache.
2. Pat into 8-inch square pan.
3. Refrigerate to set.
4. Top with Ganache, return to refrigerator to set chocolate.
5. Cut into squares.

Earl Grey Chocolate Terrine

*T*he idea for this recipe was hatched while photographing one of Minneapolis's top chefs teach a cooking class. Vincent Fran-coual amazed and amused his class with tantalizing recipes and his charming personality.

One of his creations for the evening was an Earl Grey Chocolate Terrine. I will admit to having a taste and immediately having to retrieve my eyeballs from the back of my head. But with 1 quart of cream, 9 egg yolks, 2 pounds of chocolate, and sugar, the recipe doesn't fit my healthy requirements. I decided to make a raw food recipe for the terrine.

Vincent infused the cream with Earl Grey tea, which is a black tea with a citrus-bergamot flavor. Think of orange and chocolate only more delicate, more perfumed, and more complex. Heaven. I asked Vincent if he minded if I took a stab at a healthy, raw version of this terrine. I am quite pleased with the results.

With a base of cashews and cacao, this dessert provides you with antioxidants, fiber, heart-healthy monounsaturated fats, copper, and magnesium.

Continued…

Earl Grey Chocolate Terrine continued...

3 tablespoons Earl Grey tea
1 ½ cups very hot water
1 ½ cups cashews, soaked and drained
⅓ cup agave nectar
⅓ cup cacao powder
*6 ounces raw cacao butter, melted**

1. Add tea to hot water. Let steep for 5 minutes, drain, and cool.
2. Place tea and cashews in high-speed blender and blend until smooth.
3. Add agave and cacao powder, blend until well combined.
4. Slowly pour in melted cacao butter. Blend until well combined.
5. Pour into any rectangular container that will unmold easily. I used a silicone mold that is 8 x 3 x 2 inches deep.
6. Freeze until solid. Dip mold briefly in hot water, un-mold. Slice into ½-inch pieces to serve. You can let this warm to room temperature; it will hold it's form.

*You can melt the cacao butter over hot water or in the dehydrator.

Holiday Fudge

MAKES 64 1-INCH PIECES.

1 recipe Almond Butter (see recipe page 194)
½ cup cacao powder
3 tablespoons agave nectar
2 tablespoons coconut oil, melted
½ cup dried cranberries, chopped
½ cup dried apricots, chopped
½ cup golden raisins
½ cup pecans, chopped

1. Make almond butter.
2. Mix in cacao powder, agave, and coconut oil.
3. Mix in dried cranberries, apricots, raisins, and pecans.
4. Press into 8-x 8-inch pan and refrigerate until set. Cut into 1-inch squares.

Hazelnut and Mint Truffles

Filling

1 cup cashews, soaked overnight, rinsed, and drained
⅓ cup agave nectar
1 cup dried coconut, unsweetened

1. Place drained cashews and agave in food processor. Process until smooth.
2. Add dried coconut and mix until well combined. A ball should form.
3. Remove half of the mixture and set aside. You will be making two different fillings.

Hazelnut Filling

½ cup hazelnuts, soaked for at least 3 hours and drained

1. Add hazelnuts to the mixture that is still in the food processor.
2. Process until nuts are chopped fine and mixture is well combined. Refrigerate for 30 minutes.

Mint Filling

½ teaspoon peppermint extract

1. Add peppermint extract to remaining mixture and mix well. Refrigerate for 30 minutes.

Filling Assembly

1. Roll fillings into 1-inch balls. Place in freezer for 1 hour. While fillings are setting up, make the raw chocolate.

Continued…

Raw Chocolate

7 ounces raw cacao butter
⅓ cup Sucanat, ground fine in coffee grinder.
3 tablespoons agave nectar
2 cups cacao powder

1. Melt cacao butter in dehydrator.
2. Place in food processor.
3. Add Sucanat, half of the cacao powder, and agave. Process until smooth.
4. Add the rest of the cacao powder and process until smooth.

Assembly

1. Take a filling ball and place a toothpick in it.
2. Dip it in the melted raw chocolate.
3. Holding the chocolate-dipped ball over the chocolate, let the extra chocolate run off. Be patient and wait until it has all dripped off. You can slowly turn the ball while it is dripping to get better coverage.
4. Holding the chocolate-covered ball upright, slide just the tip of a fork under the ball and very carefully slide the ball onto a nonstick sheet. Repeat until all filling balls are covered. Place back in refrigerator to set chocolate.

Chocolate-Covered Strawberry Macaroons

2 cups dried coconut, unsweetened
½ cup almond flour
¼ cup coconut butter, softened
¼ cup maple syrup
¼ cup agave nectar
pinch Himalayan salt
1 cup diced strawberries

1. Dice strawberries and set aside.
2. Mix the rest of the ingredients together.
3. Stir in diced strawberries.
4. Dehydrate at 145 degrees for 45 minutes, reduce heat, and finish dehydration (3–5 more hours) at 115 degrees.

Chocolate

½ cup cacao powder
½ cup agave nectar
¼ cup raw cacao butter, melted

1. Whisk all ingredients together.
2. While still warm, dip macaroons.
3. Chill to set.

Lemon-Glazed Fruit and Custard

SERVES 4

I am often asked where I get the inspiration for my raw food recipes. Honestly, it comes from my past food life. My classical French-cooking, gourmet-wine-pairing, foie-gras-eating life. I love food. I love all kinds of food. While my love of food hasn't diminished, my priority is now for healthy, raw food. Food that gives me the highest nutritional value.

Sometimes inspiration strikes when I see something that looks delicious, but not good for me. I was having lunch with a friend, and one of the desserts on the menu was a meringue topped with fruit and a lemon glaze. It sounded so wonderful, I had to do a raw version. No crunchy meringue, but a beautiful vanilla-custard cloud with strawberries and blueberries, topped off with a tasty, tangy lemon glaze. Enjoy!

Vanilla Custard

1 vanilla bean
2 cups cashews, soaked overnight, rinsed, and drained
1 young Thai coconut, flesh from
¼ cup coconut water, from young coconut
¾ cup coconut butter, softened
½ cup agave nectar

1. Split vanilla bean and scrape out insides.
2. Place all ingredients including vanilla in high-speed blender. Blend until smooth. You will have to be patient and use the plunger to get a really smooth consistency. Refrigerate.

Continued...

Lemon-Glazed Fruit and Custard continued...

Lemon Glaze

¼ cup coconut butter, softened
2 tablespoons agave nectar
1 tablespoon lemon juice
2 teaspoons lemon zest

1. Mix all ingredients together. This will start to set up, so make it at the last minute. If it does, you can gently warm it to get it back to a liquid.

Assembly

1 cup blueberries
1 cup strawberries
1 orange, zest from
Vanilla Custard
Lemon Glaze

1. Place a couple of spoonfuls of Custard on the plate.
2. Top with berries. Spoon Lemon Glaze on top. Sprinkle with orange zest.

Orange Chocolate "Cheesecake"

Crust

1 cup almonds
¼ cup cacao powder
3 dates

1. Combine all ingredients in food processor. Process until ground fine. Mixture should hold together when pressed. If it doesn't, add water 1 tablespoon at a time until texture is achieved.
2. Set aside ¼ cup of mixture. Press remaining into bottom of 6-inch springform pan. Place in refrigerator.

Filling

3 oranges (make sure you have very good oranges)
⅔ cup agave nectar
2 ½ cups cashews, soaked overnight, rinsed, and drained
¾ cup coconut butter, softened
½ teaspoon orange extract (food grade)

1. Grate the zest off of all the oranges. You should have at least 3 tablespoons. Be careful to only get the orange part as the pith (the white) is bitter.
2. Squeeze the juice out of all the oranges. You should have about ⅔ cup.
3. Place cashews, agave, coconut butter, zest, extract, and orange juice in food processor and process until very smooth.
4. Pour over crust, sprinkle extra crust on top, and refrigerate for at least 4 hours before serving.

Hazelnut Chocolate Mousse

2 avocados
½ cup hazelnut butter
1 cup hazelnut milk
¾ cup cacao powder
½ cup agave nectar

1. Place all ingredients in food processor. Process until very smooth.
2. Refrigerate before serving. Top with grated hazelnuts, if desired.

Hazelnut Milk

1 cup hazelnuts, soaked for 3 hours, rinsed, and drained
3 cups water

1. Place hazelnuts and water in a high-speed blender. Blend very well. Strain through nut-milk bag.

Hazelnut Butter

2 cups hazelnuts
2 tablespoons olive oil

1. Follow instructions for Almond Butter on page 194. Hazelnut butter takes longer, so you will want to add a little olive oil towards the end of processing.

OMG Pecan Bars

I love creating raw food recipes. Most of my inspiration comes from my own cravings and recipes I made before going raw. When my girls were little, I snagged a recipe for turtle bars from a great restaurant in Santa Fe. It quickly became one of our favorites. Later, a recipe from The Barefoot Contessa for pecan bars became an obsession. But with 2 pounds of butter, tons of sugar, and cream, it is completely off of my list. That doesn't mean I don't think about it once in a while, so a raw version was bound to happen sooner or later!

Using elements from both recipes (pecan bars and a ganache) this recipe came together beautifully. A tasty crust made from cashews and almonds (that resembles more of a short bread crust than a raw food recipe crust), filling from raw honey and coconut butter and a layer of pecans and ganache. All I could say when I tasted them was... oh my gosh. What is really amazing about these bars is that no one would ever guess that they are raw. Made from healthy ingredients and no dehydrator required, these simple bars will impress everyone you make them for!

Crust
½ cup cashews
½ cup almonds
3 tablespoons coconut oil, melted

1. Process cashews to make cashew flour. I did this in the dry container of the high-speed blender. Be careful not to overprocess. You want a light, fluffy flour, not butter.
2. Process almonds to make flour.
3. Combine cashew flour, almond flour, and melted coconut oil.
4. Press into 8- x 8-inch pan and place in refrigerator.

*Chef's Note: These are very sweet. A little bit goes a long way.

Continued...

OMG Pecan Bars continued...

Filling

¾ cup raw honey or agave nectar
¾ cup coconut butter, softened
3 tablespoons maple syrup
1 ½ cups pecans

Ganache

(see recipe page 203)

Assembly

1. Whisk together honey, coconut butter, and maple syrup.
2. Spread pecans over crust.
3. Pour filling mixture over pecans.
4. Spoon Ganache over top to create a swirl pattern.
5. Refrigerate to set. You will want to keep these refrigerated.

Macaroons Three Ways

Basic Macaroon Recipe

2 cups dried coconut, unsweetened
½ cup almond flour
¼ cup coconut butter, softened
¼ cup maple syrup
¼ cup agave nectar
1 vanilla bean
pinch Himalayan salt

1. Mix all ingredients together. For Vanilla Macaroons, use recipe as is.

Cinnamon Macadamia Macaroons

Add to basic recipe:
1 teaspoon cinnamon
½ cup macadamia nuts, coarsely chopped.

Strawberry Macaroons

Add to basic recipe:
½ cup chopped strawberries

Assembly

1. Drop in tablespoon mounds on dehydrator screens.
2. Dehydrate for 1 hour at 145 degrees, then for 12–20 hours at 115 degrees (depends on how moist you want your centers).
    The strawberry macaroons should be refrigerated in an airtight container.

Pluot Tart

MAKES 4 FOUR-INCH TARTS

Crust

1 ½ cups almonds, soaked and dried
2 tablespoons coconut oil, melted

1. Place almonds in food processor and process until fine.
2. Add coconut oil and pulse until well combined.
3. Press into 4 4-inch tart pans with removable bottoms, or 1 8-inch tart shell.
4. Refrigerate.

Continued...

Pluot Tart continued...

Filling

1 cup cashews, soaked and drained
1 cup water
¾ cup coconut oil, softened
2 teaspoons cinnamon
½ teaspoon ginger
¼ teaspoon cloves
⅓ cup agave nectar

1. Place cashews and water in high-speed blender and process until very smooth.
2. Add coconut oil, cinnamon, ginger, cloves, and agave. Blend.

Assembly

2 pluots, sliced (can substitute plums)

1. Pour filling mixture into refrigerated tart shells.
2. Arrange sliced pluots on top of filled tart shells.
3. Refrigerate until firm.

Raw Pumpkin Pie

Crust

2 cups pecans
4 dates, soaked until soft

1. Put pecans into food processor with dates. Process until well ground.
2. Press into 8-inch pie plate. Refrigerate.

Filling

1 medium sugar pumpkin (about 5 cups), chopped*
3 cups water (divided)
⅓ cup agave nectar
¼ cup maple syrup
½ cup coconut butter, softened
½ cup cashews, soaked overnight, rinsed, and drained
2 teaspoons cinnamon
½ teaspoon nutmeg
½ teaspoon ginger
¼ teaspoon cloves

*The day before you will start preparing the pumpkin. This is important because if you used the pumpkin completely raw, it would have a very unpleasant, starchy quality to it.

1. Peel the pumpkin and slice in half. Slice into 1-inch slices. Chop the slices into pieces that are about ⅛ inch thick. The pieces will look like 1-inch squares that are ⅛ inch thick.

Continued…

2. Place on dehydrator screens and dehydrate at 115 degrees for about 3–4 hours. Make sure you remove them before they are hard!
3. Place dehydrated pumpkin in a bowl. Cover with 2 cups of the water and let sit for about 3 hours. You can do this the night before and just put it in the refrigerator and leave it. Soak the cashews and dates at the same time and you will be ready to rock in the morning!

Filling

1. In the food processor, place all ingredients except the remaining 1 cup water and cashews.
2. Process until it becomes a mash.
3. Add the cashews and process until well mixed.
4. Transfer half the mixture to high-speed blender. Add ½-cup water and blend until smooth. This will require some patience and the plunger but the results are well worth it.
5. Repeat with remaining filling and ½-cup water.
6. Mix the two batches together.

Assembly

1. Spoon into the crust.
2. Refrigerate for at least 3-4 hours before serving.

Strawberry Basil Ice Cream

Basil Cream

2 cups cashews, soaked overnight, rinsed, and drained
2 cups water
handful fresh basil (¼ cup packed tightly)

1. Place cashews and water in high-speed blender. Process until very smooth.
2. Bruise the basil (crush it in your hand to start releasing the oils).
3. Stir into cream, place in container, and refrigerate for 24 hours, stirring occasionally.
4. Strain (a colander works the best as this is quite thick).

Ice Cream

2 cups Basil Cream
½ cup Brazil Nut Milk (see page 5)
½ cup agave nectar
1 cup strawberries, chopped

1. Combine Basil Cream, Brazil Nut Milk, and agave.
2. Freeze according to manufacturer's instructions. (You can also freeze in the freezer, scraping occasionally while freezing.)
3. Remove from ice cream maker and stir in chopped strawberries.
4. Place in container (I use glass) to finish off freezing.

Raw Strawberry Coconut Cream Pie

$\mathcal{S}$ummer and strawberries, what a great combination. One summer, a friend of mine dropped off a very large box of strawberries and the fun began. I had spinach-strawberry balsamic salads, put strawberries in green drinks, and just ate them by the dozens! When I noticed that the rest of the strawberries needed to be used, I decided to put together a recipe for a strawberry cream pie. The crust is a delicious combination of macadamia nuts and almonds with coconut, while the filling is a light, healthy combination of cashews and coconut meat, plus a few more ingredients. The special surprise is the layer of cacao that lines the crust. This recipe uses an 8-inch pie plate.

Crust

½ cup macadamia nuts
1 cup almonds
½ cup dried coconut, unsweetened
2 tablespoons coconut oil, melted
2 tablespoons agave nectar

1. Place macadamias and almonds in food processor. Process until a coarse meal is achieved.
2. Add the coconut oil, coconut, and agave. Pulse until blended.
3. Spread into an 8-inch pie plate. The crust will be sticky, so it helps to do this with wet hands. Refrigerate.

Continued...

Chocolate Sauce

½ cup cacao powder
½ cup agave nectar
¼ cup coconut oil (melted over warm water)
1 vanilla bean

1. Split vanilla bean in half and, with a table knife, scrape all the pulp out of the inside of the bean.
2. Place the vanilla bean scrapings and the rest of the ingredients into a high-speed blender. Blend for 2 minutes.
3. Spread a layer (you will have quite a bit left over) on the bottom of the crust. Place in refrigerator to set.

Filling

2 cups cashews, soaked overnight, rinsed, and drained
1 cup young Thai coconut flesh
1 vanilla bean
¼ cup coconut oil, softened
¼ cup water from young coconut
2 cups strawberries, sliced
flaked dried coconut

1. Split the young coconut and reserve ¼-cup water. Scrape out the filling.
2. Combine all ingredients in high-speed blender. Process until smooth.
3. Place filling in bowl and stir in sliced strawberries.
4. Pile filling into chocolate-lined crust, top with flaked coconut, and refrigerate until set.

Zucchini Cacao Cookies

3 cups zucchini
2 cups raw oat flour
¾ cup cacao powder
2 apples, cored and quartered
½ cup agave nectar
⅓ cup water
¼ cup olive oil

1. Grate zucchini and set aside.
2. Mix together cacao powder and oat flour. Set aside.
3. Place apples in food processor with agave, water, and olive oil. Process until smooth.
4. Stir together flour mixture and apple mixture.
5. Add to grated zucchini and stir until well combined.
6. Drop by spoonful onto nonstick dehydrator sheets. Flatten slightly.
7. Dehydrate at 145 degrees for 30 minutes then reduce heat to 115 degrees and dry for 4 hours. Remove from nonstick sheets and continue to dry until done (approximately 4 more hours).

Tropical Biscotti

1 ½ cups almond flour
1 cup almonds
1 cup dried coconut, unsweetened
½ cup agave nectar
½ cup dried apricots
½ cup dried pineapple
½ cup currants
1 large orange, juice and zest from

1. Hand chop or roughly chop in food processor, the apricots and the pineapple. Set aside.
2. Place almonds in food processor and pulse until a coarse meal is achieved.
3. Add almond flour and coconut. Pulse until just combined.
4. Add agave and pulse until combined. At this point, remove from processor and place in bowl.
5. Add orange juice and zest, combine by hand.
6. Mix in chopped fruit and currants.
7. Form into biscotti-shaped loaves and dehydrate at 115 degrees for 8 hours. Cut into ¾-inch slices and return to dehydrator until desired dryness is achieved. This is a moist dough, so don't be surprised if it takes a little longer to dehydrate. I like to leave a little moisture in and store in the refrigerator.

White Chocolate, Dark Chocolate Raspberry Tart

*Y*ears ago, one of my family's favorite desserts was a white chocolate, raspberry, and chocolate tart. I thought about it and decided to make a raw version for a 4th of July celebration at my friend Kim's house. I was the only raw food person there, but I sure wasn't the only person who loved the dessert. It was a huge success. If you want a light crust, you will have to peel the almonds. This is actually very easy once they have been soaked, as the skins pop right off. This beautiful dessert looks like you spent hours in the kitchen but actually comes together very quickly.

Crust

1 cup almonds, soaked overnight, rinsed, and drained
¼ cup coconut oil, melted

1. Process almonds in food processor until finely ground.
2. Add coconut oil and pulse until well combined.
3. Press mixture in the bottom of an 8-inch tart pan.
4. Place in refrigerator.

Continued...

White Chocolate, Dark Chocolate Raspberry Tart continued...

Filling

2 cups cashews, soaked
⅓ cup agave nectar
½ cup cacao butter, melted
⅓ cup coconut oil, melted
1 teaspoon vanilla
2 pints raspberries

1. Blend cashews, agave, cacao butter, coconut oil, and vanilla in food processor.
2. Process until very smooth. You can also use a high-speed blender.
3. Spread a thin layer of the filling on the crust.
4. Place a layer of raspberries over the filling. Pack them tightly.
5. Pour the rest of the filling mixture over raspberries.
6. Refrigerate.
7. Top with layer of Chocolate Ganache.

Chocolate Ganache

½ cup cacao powder
½ cup agave nectar
¼ cup coconut butter, softened

1. Whisk all ingredients together until smooth.

Ingredient List

Almond Flour: There are a few ways you can make almond flour. You can dehydrate the pulp from almond milk or grind almonds in the food processor or high-speed blender. It you use the blender/food processor method, it is better to use almonds that have been soaked and dehydrated as they will release oil and make a better flour. Just make sure you stop before you get almond butter.

Agave Nectar: Agave nectar has come under a lot of scrutiny lately. I happen to like agave for a few reasons. First, a good agave is the organic sap from the agave cactus that has been reduced to a syrup using low heat and enzymes. One thing I really like about agave is that a little goes a long way. It is also low glycemic. It is important to remember that agave is a sugar and should be used as such, sparingly. I like Xagave. You can find out more at www.Xagave.com

Chia Seeds: The little black seeds that grow "hair" on the famous chia pets are actually incredibly nutritious. You will want to mail order seeds or get them at your co-op to make sure they are food grade. Chia seeds are very rich in omega-3 fatty acids, even more so than flax seeds. They are very rich in antioxidants and store much better than flax. They also don't have to be ground to release their nutrient goodness.

Raw Flaked Oats and Oat Flour: Raw organic flaked oats and oat flour are made from organic oat groats without heat. Oats can be a very healthy addition to your diet. Full of fiber, great for your heart, chlosterol reducing, I get my raw oats and oat flour from Sunrise Flour Mills. You can find them here: www.SunriseFlourMill.com

Maple Syrup: Maple syrup is not a raw ingredient. It is the sap from the maple tree that has been reduced over high heat. It is used often in raw food recipes for flavor and texture.

Nutritional Yeast: Made from the yeast that grows on molasses, it is full of B-vitamins and other nutrients. Not raw but used to flavor raw food recipes.

Sprouted Wheat Berries: To sprout wheat berries, soak over-night in pure water. The next morning, drain the berries and rinse 3–4 times a day until little tails sprout. You can use them when the tails are as long as the grain. They are packed with nutrients at this point.

Nuts: There are many different nuts that we use in raw food recipes. Nuts are not interchangeable. Cashews have a very creamy texture while almonds will be more grainy. Most nuts will be soaked overnight and used wet. There are two reasons for this. One is to release the digestive enzyme inhibitors, the second is for texture. If soaked nuts are not required, make sure your nuts are dry. You can presoak and dehydrate them so that they are ready for recipes. It is important to keep your nuts fresh as they have oils in them that can go rancid.

Flax Seeds: It is important to buy fresh flax seeds and grind your own when ground flax is called for. Flax is very unstable and once ground, the oils go rancid very quickly. To get the most benefit, make sure you use fresh flax.

Himalayan Salt: I love Himalayan salt. It is pure, full of minerals, incredibly tasty and you need just a pinch to flavor your food. You will notice it is used throughout this cookbook.

Smoked Paprika: I get this from Penzeys Spices at www.Penzeys.com

Sucanat: It is a form of whole cane sugar juice which retains the molasses. It is essentially dried cane sugar juice. It is dried with heat so not raw.

Susan's Story

*H*aving been involved with food and wine for years as a trained sommelier, gourmet food and fine wines were a part of my everyday lifestyle. Meeting and and working with many top chefs and studying classical French cooking, along with many other cuisines, inspired my passion and creativity for food. It also led me down a path to excess weight, general fatigue, and other symptoms that I knew were associated with my diet. My body was seriously rebelling and I needed to do something about it.

Then I found raw. It was exciting to find a whole new way to prepare and eat food. Exploring the world of raw food was intriguing and creative. There were new things to learn at every turn. I tried some of my own recipes but experienced a lot of failure, so I just learned how to prepare raw food using every cookbook I could get my hands on. Reading about raw, the health benefits, and the principles of this way of eating, became an obsession.

I became 100 percent raw. It was amazing. I lost weight, had more energy than I had ever had, and the best part was the mental clarity that I began to experience. My health issues resolved themselves and I felt better than I had for years.

But all journeys have their bumps in the road. Minnesota winters are very cold and long. Stress was building up in my life from other sources and I defaulted back to my "comfort" food. All the consequences of what I was eating became glaringly obvious as I gained weight, experienced more fatigue, and lost my focus. Knowing full well that all of the symptoms I was having were directly related to what I was eating, when spring hit, I decided to dedicate myself to raw again.

This time, I did it differently. Food is a sensory experience. My greatest desire was to create food that not only tasted wonderful, but also was beautiful to look at. I believe in presentation and that it is an important part of the dining experience. Having fallen off of the wagon also gave me insights on how to incorporate raw back into my life... striving for 80–90 percent this time, not 100 percent. With a little patience, planning, and some transitional recipes, I found it is easy to avoid the pitfalls that tempted me and took my raw food creations in a completely new direction. Easy, beautiful food that tastes great and reminds me of the food I was accustomed to eating. Eating well is one of the best gifts that we can give ourselves and our loved ones. This is where my greatest success has grown from. Translating people's favorite foods into entirely healthy, easy, raw feasts.

Having the unique background with food has enabled me to bring many of the traditional ways of making food into the raw world. My creativity is establishing a whole new raw. Balancing flavors, tastes, and mouth feel, my expectations of the way food should taste and look are very high. People are often heard saying, "I can't believe this is raw" and "I can feed my family this, they will eat it!"

It is said that 60 percent of our illness in this country is caused by the SAD (Standard American Diet). Our current way of eating is not only making us sick, it is also quickly depleting our planet of its resources in ways that are completely unnecessary. It is time to bring a new mindset to the masses. I will show you ways to a more nutritional way of eating that doesn't require you to give up the flavor and beauty of food!

Photos:

(all photos are listed from left to right, top to bottom)

Come visit us at
www.rawmazing.com